Healing Your Inner Child

Live with Awareness, Embrace Your Dignity, Overcome Trauma and Discover Your Own Better Version

By

Deborah F. Blane

© Copyright 2023 by Deborah F. Blane - All rights reserved.

This document is geared towards providing exact and reliable information in regard to the topic and issue covered. The publication is sold with the idea that the publisher is not required to render accounting, officially permitted, or otherwise qualified services. If advice is necessary, legal or professional, a practiced individual in the profession should be ordered.

- From a Declaration of Principles, which was accepted and approved equally by a Committee of the American Bar Association and a Committee of Publishers and Associations.

In no way is it legal to reproduce, duplicate, or transmit any part of this document in either electronic means or in printed format. Recording of this publication is strictly prohibited, and any storage of this document is not allowed unless with written permission from the publisher. All rights reserved.

The information provided herein is stated to be truthful and consistent in that any liability, in terms of inattention or otherwise, by any usage or abuse of any policies, processes, or directions contained within is the solitary and utter responsibility of the recipient reader. Under no circumstances will any legal responsibility or blame be held against the publisher for any reparation, damages, or monetary loss due to the information herein, either directly or indirectly.

Respective authors own all copyrights not held by the publisher.

The information herein is offered for informational purposes solely and is universal as so. The presentation of the information is without a contract or any type of guarantee assurance. The trademarks that are used are without any consent, and the publication of the trademark is without permission or backing by the trademark owner. All trademarks and brands within this book are for clarifying purposes only and are owned by the owners themselves, not affiliated with this document.

Table of Contents

Introduction 6

Chapter 1: Understanding The Inner Child 7

    1.1 Importance Of Healing The Inner Child 7

1.2 What Is The Inner Child? 8

1.3 How Childhood Experiences Impact The Inner Child 10

1.4 Recognizing The Signs Of An Unhealed Inner Child 13

1.5 Benefits Of Healing The Inner Child 16

1.6 Workbook: Reflection Exercises For Identifying Your Inner Child's Wounds 20

Chapter 2: Reconnecting With The Inner Child 23

2.1 Rebuilding The Connection With Your Inner Child 23

2.2 Creating A Safe Space For The Inner Child 24

2.3 Listening And Validating The Inner Child's Emotions 26

2.4 Techniques For Nurturing Your Inner Child 29

2.5 Workbook: Writing Exercises For Initiating A Dialogue With Your Inner Child 33

Chapter 3: Healing Childhood Wounds 36

3.1 Exploring And Understanding Childhood Wounds 36

3.2 Processing And Releasing Emotional Pain 39

3.3 Techniques For Healing Childhood Wounds 42

3.4 Forgiveness And Compassion Towards Yourself And Others 46

3.5 Workbook: Guided Exercises For Healing Specific Childhood Wounds 50

Chapter 4: Reparenting The Inner Child 53

4.1 Becoming Your Own Loving Parent 53

4.2 Providing The Care And Support Your Inner Child Needs 56

4.3 Setting Healthy Boundaries And Nurturing Self-Care Practices 58

4.4 Cultivating Self-Compassion And Self-Love 60

4.5 Workbook: Daily Practices For Reparenting Your Inner Child 63

Chapter 5: Inner Child Integration 65

5.1 Integrating The Healed Inner Child Into Your Adult Self 65

5.2 Embracing The Gifts And Strengths Of Your Inner Child 68

5.3 Living Authentically And Joyfully 71

5.4 Nurturing Ongoing Inner Child Growth And Healing 73

5.5 Reflecting On Your Inner Child Healing Journey 75

5.6 Encouragement And Next Steps 77

5.7 Workbook: Creating A Personalized Inner Child Integration Plan 80

Conclusion 83

Introduction

Welcome to "Unlocking the Healing of the Inner Child." This book is a guide to understanding and transforming the wounds of your inner child, offering you the tools and insights to embark on a profound healing journey.

The inner child represents the essence of who we were in our early years—the innocent, vulnerable, and curious part of ourselves. It is within this inner child that our deepest wounds and unresolved traumas reside, shaping our beliefs, behaviors, and emotional patterns as adults.

The healing of the inner child is a powerful and transformative process that allows us to reconnect with and nurture this wounded part of ourselves. By addressing these wounds and providing the love, care, and validation our inner child needs, we can create a solid foundation for personal growth, emotional well-being, and fulfilling relationships.

In this book, we will explore the concept of the inner child, delve into the impact of childhood experiences on our adult lives, and understand the signs of an unhealed inner child. We will uncover the many benefits of healing the inner child, including increased self-awareness, emotional resilience, and the ability to form healthier connections with others.

Throughout each chapter, you will find a combination of informative explanations, practical exercises, and insightful reflection prompts. These tools are designed to facilitate your healing journey, allowing you to gain deeper insights into your inner child's wounds, reconnect with their needs and emotions, and develop a compassionate and nurturing relationship with yourself.

By embarking on the path of healing your inner child, you are embarking on a journey of self-discovery, self-compassion, and self-love. It is an act of courage, resilience, and profound transformation. Remember, you are not alone on this journey. This book will serve as your trusted companion, offering guidance, support, and inspiration every step of the way.

So, let us begin the process of unlocking the healing of your inner child. Together, we will embark on a journey of profound self-discovery, healing, and transformation that will empower you to live a more authentic, joyful, and fulfilling life.

Chapter 1: Understanding The Inner Child

In this chapter, we will dive deep into the concept of the inner child and its significance in our lives. Understanding the inner child is crucial to unraveling the root causes of our emotional patterns, behavior, and beliefs as adults. By gaining insights into the inner child, we can begin the journey of healing and nurturing this wounded part of ourselves.

1.1 Importance Of Healing The Inner Child

Healing the inner child is a therapeutic process that involves acknowledging, understanding, and addressing the wounds, traumas, and unmet needs of one's childhood. The concept of the inner child recognizes that our childhood experiences shape our adult lives, and unresolved issues from the past can continue to impact our emotional, mental, and even physical well-being. By healing the inner child, individuals can experience personal growth, emotional resilience, and a deeper sense of self-compassion. Let's explore the importance of healing the inner child in detail:

Understanding unresolved childhood issues

Many of us carry unresolved issues from our childhood, such as neglect, abuse, abandonment, or emotional pain. These experiences can lead to various negative patterns in our adult lives, including low self-esteem, relationship difficulties, self-sabotaging behaviors, and emotional reactivity. Healing the inner child involves identifying and understanding these unresolved issues to break free from their influence.

Emotional healing

Unresolved childhood issues often create emotional wounds that affect our emotional well-being as adults. Healing the inner child allows us to process and release pent-up emotions such as anger, sadness, fear, or grief that were suppressed or denied during childhood. By addressing and healing these emotions, we can experience emotional liberation, increased self-awareness, and emotional resilience.

Self-compassion and self-acceptance

The healing process involves developing self-compassion and self-acceptance toward our inner child. Many individuals tend to be self-critical or hold themselves to unrealistically high standards due to early experiences of rejection or criticism. By acknowledging and embracing our inner child with love and compassion, we can cultivate a healthier self-image, develop a sense of self-worth, and foster a more positive relationship with ourselves.

Breaking destructive patterns

Unresolved childhood issues often contribute to the development of unhealthy patterns and coping mechanisms. These can manifest as addictive behaviors, self-destructive habits, or toxic relationship dynamics. Healing the inner child helps us gain insight into these patterns, allowing us to consciously choose healthier alternatives and break free from self-defeating cycles.

Improved relationships

Our relationships as adults can be significantly impacted by unresolved childhood issues. Unhealed wounds can lead to difficulties in forming and maintaining healthy connections, as well as patterns of codependency, distrust, or emotional unavailability. By healing our inner child, we can enhance our ability to form secure attachments, communicate effectively, and establish healthier boundaries in our relationships.

Rediscovering joy and playfulness

The healing process involves reconnecting with the joy, spontaneity, and playfulness that may have been stifled during childhood. Engaging with our inner child allows us to tap into our creativity, imagination, and curiosity, which can contribute to a more fulfilling and vibrant adult life.

Personal growth and self-actualization

Healing the inner child is a transformative journey that promotes personal growth and self-actualization. By addressing and resolving unresolved childhood issues, individuals can develop a deeper understanding of themselves, gain clarity about their values and aspirations, and unlock their full potential.

1.2 What Is The Inner Child?

The inner child refers to a concept within psychology and therapy that represents the childlike aspects of our personality, emotions, and experiences that we carry with us into adulthood. It represents the child we once were and encompasses our early memories, emotions, needs, and beliefs that were formed during our formative years. Here is a detailed explanation of the inner child:

Origin and development

The inner child concept is rooted in the belief that our childhood experiences significantly shape our adult lives. During our early years, we go through various stages of physical, emotional, and cognitive development. Our interactions with caregivers, family dynamics, societal influences, and the environment around us contribute to the formation of our beliefs, emotions, and coping mechanisms.

Emotional and vulnerable aspects

The inner child represents our emotional and vulnerable self. It encompasses our deepest feelings, needs, and desires, including the need for love, acceptance, validation, and safety. It also includes the experiences of pain, fear, abandonment, neglect, or any other emotional wounds we may have suffered during childhood.

Unresolved issues and trauma

The inner child carries unresolved issues, traumas, and unmet needs from the past. These can include experiences of physical or emotional abuse, neglect, parental divorce, loss, or any other adverse childhood experiences. When these issues remain unaddressed or unhealed, they can continue to influence our thoughts, emotions, behaviors, and relationships in adulthood.

Impact on adult life

The unresolved wounds of the inner child can manifest in various ways in our adult lives. They can contribute to low self-esteem, self-sabotaging behaviors, perfectionism, people-pleasing tendencies, difficulties in forming and maintaining healthy relationships, emotional reactivity, and patterns of self-criticism or self-sabotage.

Healing and integration

Healing the inner child involves recognizing, validating, and addressing the unmet needs and wounds of the past. It requires developing a nurturing and compassionate relationship with our inner child, acknowledging the pain and emotions associated with past experiences, and providing the love, care, and support that may have been lacking during childhood. Through inner child work and therapeutic techniques, individuals can heal their inner child, release emotional pain, and integrate these aspects into their adult selves.

Inner child and self-expression

The inner child is also associated with creativity, playfulness, spontaneity, and joy. As adults, reconnecting with our inner child can unlock our creativity, imagination, and ability to experience simple pleasures. Engaging in activities that nurture our inner child, such as art, music, dancing, or playful exploration, can foster personal growth, self-expression, and a sense of vitality.

Re-parenting the inner child

Re-parenting the inner child involves providing the care, understanding, and support that may have been lacking during childhood. It means becoming the loving and nurturing parent to our inner child, meeting their emotional needs, and developing a sense of self-compassion and self-acceptance. This process involves cultivating self-awareness, self-care practices, and engaging in therapeutic interventions that promote healing and growth.

1.3 How Childhood Experiences Impact The Inner Child

Childhood experiences have a profound impact on the development and well-being of the inner child. These experiences shape the way we perceive ourselves, others, and the world around us. Here is a detailed explanation of how childhood experiences impact the inner child:

Attachment and bonding

The quality of the early attachment bond between a child and their primary caregivers significantly influences the development of the inner child. Secure attachment, characterized by consistent emotional responsiveness and a sense of safety and trust, promotes healthy emotional development. In contrast, insecure attachment patterns, such as avoidant, anxious, or disorganized attachment, can lead to emotional insecurity and difficulties in forming and maintaining healthy relationships.

The emotional and physical environment

The emotional and physical environment in which a child grows up plays a crucial role in shaping the inner child. Positive and nurturing environments that provide love, support, and emotional validation contribute to healthy emotional development. Conversely, environments characterized by neglect, abuse, or inconsistent care can result in emotional wounds, low self-esteem, and difficulties in regulating emotions.

Trauma and adverse experiences

Childhood trauma, whether it be physical, emotional, or sexual abuse, neglect, witnessing violence, or other adverse experiences, can deeply impact the inner child. Trauma disrupts a child's sense of safety, trust, and self-worth and can result in various psychological and emotional difficulties that persist into adulthood. Unresolved trauma can manifest as anxiety, depression, post-traumatic stress disorder (PTSD), or other mental health issues.

Beliefs and cognitive development

Childhood experiences shape the beliefs and cognitive frameworks through which we perceive ourselves and the world. Positive experiences and supportive environments foster a sense of self-worth, confidence, and positive beliefs about oneself and others. Conversely, negative experiences, criticism, or rejection can lead to negative self-beliefs, self-doubt, and distorted perceptions of oneself and others.

Emotional regulation and coping mechanisms

The inner child's ability to regulate emotions and develop healthy coping mechanisms is influenced by childhood experiences. Children who grow up in environments where their emotions are validated, understood, and supported learn healthy ways to express and regulate their emotions. In contrast, children who experience invalidation, suppression, or punishment of their emotions may develop maladaptive coping strategies such as emotional repression, aggression, or avoidance.

Core emotional needs

The inner child carries unmet core emotional needs from childhood. These needs include love, care, acceptance, safety, validation, and belonging. When these needs are not adequately met, the inner child may develop a sense of emotional emptiness, longing, or feelings of being unworthy. The unmet needs of the inner child can manifest in adulthood as a persistent search for validation, people-pleasing tendencies, or difficulties in establishing healthy boundaries.

Cognitive and social development

Childhood experiences significantly impact cognitive and social development, which in turn shape the inner child. Positive experiences that promote cognitive stimulation, social interaction, and exploration foster healthy cognitive and social skills. On the other hand, adverse experiences or a lack of supportive environments can hinder cognitive and social development, leading to difficulties in academic performance, social relationships, and self-confidence.

Core beliefs and self-concept

Childhood experiences contribute to the formation of core beliefs about oneself, others, and the world. Positive experiences, such as receiving love, support, and encouragement, tend to foster positive core beliefs and a healthy self-concept. However, negative experiences, such as criticism, rejection, or being made to feel inadequate, can lead to negative core beliefs and a distorted self-image. These negative beliefs can persist into adulthood and influence how the inner child perceives and interacts with the world.

Patterns of behavior and relationships

Childhood experiences influence the patterns of behavior and relationships that the inner child develops. For example, children who grow up in an environment characterized by conflict or abuse may internalize unhealthy relationship dynamics and exhibit similar patterns in their adult relationships. Similarly, children who experience neglect or emotional unavailability may struggle with forming secure and trusting connections in their adult relationships. Understanding these patterns allows individuals to identify and change unhealthy behaviors and relationship dynamics.

Emotional intelligence and expression

Childhood experiences significantly impact emotional intelligence and the ability to express emotions. Children who are encouraged to identify, express, and regulate their emotions in a healthy way tend to develop higher emotional intelligence. On the other hand, children who grow up in environments where emotions are suppressed or invalidated may struggle with emotional expression and regulation in adulthood. Healing the inner child involves relearning healthy emotional expression and developing emotional intelligence.

Cognitive distortions and negative thinking patterns

Childhood experiences can contribute to the development of cognitive distortions and negative thinking patterns that affect the inner child's perception of themselves and the world. For example, if a child constantly experiences criticism, they may develop a negative thinking pattern where they constantly berate themselves or expect failure. These cognitive distortions

can contribute to low self-esteem, anxiety, and depression in adulthood. Healing the inner child involves challenging and replacing these negative thought patterns with healthier, more positive ones.

Resilience and coping skills

The way children are supported and guided through challenging experiences plays a crucial role in the development of resilience and healthy coping skills. Children who have positive role models, access to support systems, and are taught effective coping strategies are more likely to develop resilience and adaptability. In contrast, children who experience chronic stress, neglect, or lack of support may struggle with resilience and resort to maladaptive coping mechanisms. Healing the inner child involves building resilience and developing healthy coping strategies to navigate life's challenges.

Limiting beliefs and self-sabotage

Childhood experiences can contribute to the formation of limiting beliefs and self-sabotaging behaviors that hinder personal growth and success. For example, if a child grows up in an environment where they are constantly told they will never amount to anything, they may internalize this belief and unknowingly self-sabotage their efforts as adults. Healing the inner child involves identifying and challenging these limiting beliefs, replacing them with empowering beliefs, and breaking free from self-sabotaging patterns.

Identity formation and a sense of purpose

Childhood experiences shape the development of identity and the sense of purpose in adulthood. Positive experiences and a supportive environment can foster a strong and authentic sense of self, while negative experiences can lead to identity confusion or a lack of clear direction. Healing the inner child involves exploring and rediscovering one's true identity, values, and passions and aligning them with a sense of purpose.

1.4 Recognizing The Signs Of An Unhealed Inner Child

Recognizing the signs of an unhealed inner child is crucial for self-awareness and initiating the healing process. Here are detailed explanations of common signs that may indicate an unhealed inner child:

Emotional reactivity

If you find yourself reacting intensely or disproportionately to certain situations or triggers, it may be a sign of an unhealed inner child. Unresolved childhood wounds can cause emotional sensitivity and reactive responses due to unmet emotional needs or past traumas.

Relationship patterns

Unhealed inner child issues can affect your relationships. You may notice patterns of codependency, seeking validation from others, difficulty establishing healthy boundaries, fear of abandonment, or a tendency to attract and repeat unhealthy relationship dynamics from your past.

Low self-esteem

An unhealed inner child often manifests persistent feelings of low self-worth, self-doubt, or self-criticism. You may struggle with a negative self-image, feelings of inadequacy, or a constant need for external validation.

People-pleasing tendencies

If you frequently prioritize others' needs and desires over your own, have difficulty saying no, or struggle with asserting your boundaries, it could be a sign of an unhealed inner child. People-pleasing often stems from a fear of rejection or abandonment, which may have originated in childhood.

Fear of vulnerability

An unhealed inner child can lead to a fear of vulnerability and intimacy. You may have difficulty expressing your true emotions, being open about your needs and desires, or forming deep connections with others due to past experiences of emotional pain or betrayal.

Self-sabotaging behaviors

Unresolved inner child wounds can manifest in self-sabotaging behaviors that hinder personal growth and success. These behaviors may include procrastination, self-destructive habits, self-sabotage in relationships or career opportunities, or persistent fear of failure.

Difficulty regulating emotions

An unhealed inner child can result in challenges with emotional regulation. You may experience intense mood swings, difficulty managing anger or sadness, or a tendency to suppress or avoid certain emotions altogether. Emotions that were not adequately addressed or validated in childhood may resurface and impact your emotional well-being as an adult.

Perfectionism and overachievement

If you constantly strive for perfection, have high self-imposed standards, or struggle with a fear of failure, it may indicate an unhealed inner child. These behaviors often stem from a deep-seated need for validation, acceptance, or love that was unmet in childhood.

Feelings of emptiness or longing

An unhealed inner child may result in a persistent sense of emptiness or a longing for something you can't quite define. You may feel like something is missing from your life or that you're constantly searching for fulfillment or validation from external sources.

Difficulty accessing joy and playfulness

If you struggle to experience joy, have a rigid or serious demeanor, or find it challenging to engage in spontaneous and playful activities, it could be an indication of an unhealed inner child.

Suppressed or neglected aspects of your inner child can inhibit your ability to tap into your natural sense of curiosity, creativity, and joy.

Avoidance of past trauma or emotions

If you find yourself avoiding or suppressing memories, emotions, or discussions related to your childhood, it may be an indication of an unhealed inner child. Unresolved trauma or painful experiences from the past can be challenging to confront, leading to avoidance or numbing behaviors as a coping mechanism.

Addictive or self-destructive behaviors

Unhealed inner child wounds can contribute to addictive or self-destructive behaviors. This can include substance abuse, overeating, excessive spending, or engaging in risky behaviors as a way to numb emotional pain or fill a void. These behaviors often serve as temporary escapes from the unresolved emotional issues of the inner child.

Chronic self-criticism

An unhealed inner child may result in a persistent inner critic that constantly berates and undermines your self-worth. You may find yourself engaging in negative self-talk, focusing on perceived flaws or mistakes, and struggling with self-acceptance. This self-critical voice often originates from internalized negative messages received during childhood.

Difficulty accessing inner child qualities

If you have trouble accessing or connecting with the qualities of joy, wonder, spontaneity, and creativity associated with the inner child, it may indicate that your inner child is unhealed. The inability to engage in playful activities, express creativity, or experience a sense of lightheartedness can be a result of past wounds that hinder the connection with your inner child.

Repetition of childhood patterns

Unresolved issues from the inner child tend to manifest as repetitive patterns in adulthood. You may find yourself recreating situations or dynamics reminiscent of your childhood experiences, even if they are unhealthy or detrimental. Recognizing these patterns can serve as a signal that your inner child requires healing and attention.

Feeling disconnected or detached

An unhealed inner child can contribute to a sense of disconnection or detachment from oneself and others. You may feel like you're merely going through the motions of life without a deep sense of authenticity or connection. This detachment can arise from unresolved emotional pain or a protective mechanism developed during childhood to cope with difficult experiences.

Fear of abandonment or rejection

If you have an intense fear of being abandoned, rejected, or left alone, it may be a sign of an unhealed inner child. Early experiences of abandonment or inconsistent care can create deep-seated fears that persist into adulthood, impacting relationships and self-confidence.

Chronic feelings of sadness or grief

Unresolved childhood experiences can lead to persistent feelings of sadness, grief, or melancholy. These emotions may stem from unmet needs, loss, or unaddressed pain from the past. If you find yourself experiencing chronic feelings of sadness without a clear cause, it could be an indication of an unhealed inner child.

1.5 Benefits Of Healing The Inner Child

Healing the inner child can have profound and far-reaching benefits for one's overall well-being and personal growth. Here are detailed explanations of the benefits of healing the inner child:

Emotional healing

Healing the inner child allows for the processing and release of unresolved emotional pain, trauma, and wounds from the past. By acknowledging and addressing these experiences, you can find emotional healing and experience a greater sense of inner peace, emotional resilience, and stability.

Self-awareness and self-discovery

The process of healing the inner child involves self-reflection, introspection, and understanding the impact of past experiences on your beliefs, behaviors, and emotions. Through this exploration, you gain a deeper understanding of yourself, your needs, and your patterns, leading to increased self-awareness and self-discovery.

Improved self-esteem and self-worth

Healing the inner child helps to cultivate a healthy sense of self-esteem and self-worth. By addressing and resolving childhood wounds, you can let go of negative beliefs about yourself and embrace a more positive self-image. This shift in self-perception allows for greater self-acceptance, self-love, and a stronger foundation of confidence and self-assurance.

Authenticity and self-expression

Healing the inner child encourages the expression of your authentic self. By reconnecting with your inner child's natural qualities of playfulness, creativity, and spontaneity, you can tap into your true essence. This leads to greater authenticity in your relationships, pursuits, and creative endeavors and allows you to express yourself more freely and genuinely.

Improved relationships

Healing the inner child positively impacts your relationships with others. By addressing past wounds and patterns, you become more aware of your own triggers, reactions, and relational dynamics. This newfound awareness enables you to communicate more effectively, establish healthy boundaries, and develop healthier patterns of relating, fostering deeper and more fulfilling connections with others.

Emotional resilience and regulation

Healing the inner child supports the development of emotional resilience and healthy emotional regulation. By addressing and healing past wounds, you become better equipped to navigate and manage your emotions. You develop healthier coping mechanisms, improve your ability to communicate and express emotions, and enhance your capacity to handle stress and adversity.

Breaking self-sabotaging patterns

The healing of the inner child helps to identify and break self-sabotaging patterns and behaviors that stem from unresolved childhood wounds. As you heal, you become more aware of self-defeating behaviors and beliefs that hinder your personal growth and success. This awareness empowers you to make conscious choices and embrace healthier patterns and behaviors that align with your goals and values.

Greater joy, playfulness, and creativity

Healing the inner child allows you to reconnect with the joy, playfulness, and creativity that may have been stifled or suppressed. By nurturing and integrating your inner child, you rediscover the ability to experience life with a sense of wonder, engage in playful activities, and tap into your innate creativity. This infusion of joy and creativity enhances your overall well-being and brings a renewed sense of vitality and inspiration to your life.

Release of limiting beliefs and patterns

Healing the inner child involves challenging and releasing limiting beliefs, negative thought patterns, and self-imposed limitations that were formed during childhood. By reframing these beliefs and replacing them with more empowering and positive ones, you open yourself up to new possibilities, expanded potential, and a greater sense of personal freedom.

Spiritual growth and connection

Healing the inner child can deepen your spiritual journey and connection. By nurturing your inner child's needs for love, acceptance, and safety, you create a solid foundation for spiritual growth. This process helps to align your inner self with your higher purpose, allowing for a more profound sense of spiritual connection and fulfillment.

Increased self-compassion

Healing the inner child involves developing self-compassion, which is the ability to treat oneself with kindness, understanding, and acceptance. By acknowledging and addressing the pain and wounds of the inner child, you learn to offer yourself the same compassion and care you would give to a loved one. This cultivates a deep sense of self-nurturing and self-acceptance.

Enhanced creativity and problem-solving

Healing the inner child unlocks your natural creativity and problem-solving abilities. As you reconnect with the playful and imaginative aspects of your inner child, you tap into a wellspring of innovative ideas and approaches. This renewed creativity can benefit various areas of your life, such as work, hobbies, and personal projects.

Resolving unmet needs

The healing of the inner child involves addressing and resolving unmet emotional, physical, and psychological needs from childhood. By giving yourself permission to acknowledge and fulfill these needs as an adult, you experience a sense of wholeness and fulfillment. This healing process allows you to reclaim aspects of yourself that may have been neglected or overlooked in the past.

Healing generational patterns

Unresolved issues from childhood often span across generations, perpetuating certain patterns and behaviors. By healing the inner child, you not only break free from these generational patterns within yourself but also contribute to the healing of future generations. Your own healing journey becomes a powerful catalyst for positive change in your family and community.

Increased resilience in the face of adversity

Healing the inner child fosters emotional resilience, which is the ability to bounce back and thrive in the face of challenges. As you address and heal past wounds, you develop a stronger sense of self and an increased capacity to cope with stress and adversity. This resilience enables you to navigate life's difficulties with greater ease and grace.

A Greater sense of purpose and meaning

Healing the inner child aligns you with your true purpose and helps you find deeper meaning in life. By addressing and healing the wounds of the past, you remove the barriers that may have prevented you from fully embracing your purpose and living a meaningful life. You gain clarity about your values, passions, and aspirations and can align your actions and choices with your authentic self.

Improved physical well-being

Healing the inner child can have positive effects on your physical health. Unresolved emotional pain and stress from childhood can manifest as physical ailments and chronic health conditions. By healing the inner child and releasing emotional blockages, you may experience improvements in physical symptoms, increased vitality, and a strengthened immune system.

Expanded capacity for love and compassion

Healing the inner child opens your heart to a greater capacity for love, compassion, and empathy. As you heal and integrate your inner child, you develop a deeper understanding of your own pain and struggles. This understanding enables you to empathize with others and cultivate meaningful connections built on love and compassion.

Freedom from past limitations

Healing the inner child liberates you from the limitations and constraints of the past. It allows you to break free from old patterns, beliefs, and traumas that may have held you back from fully embracing your potential. With an unburdened and healed inner child, you can step into a future filled with possibilities and create the life you truly desire.

Transformation and personal growth

Ultimately, healing the inner child is a transformative journey that leads to profound personal growth. It empowers you to release the weight of the past, embrace your authentic self, and step into a more empowered and fulfilling life. Through this process, you develop resilience, self-compassion, and a deep understanding of yourself, which fosters ongoing personal and spiritual evolution.

1.6 Workbook: Reflection Exercises For Identifying Your Inner Child's Wounds

This workbook is designed to guide you through a series of reflection exercises aimed at identifying and understanding the wounds of your inner child. By engaging in these exercises, you will gain insights into your past experiences, emotions, and beliefs that may have shaped your inner child's wounds. This awareness is a crucial first step in the healing process.

Exercises	Explanation
Journaling Your Early Memories	Begin by setting aside dedicated time in a quiet and comfortable space. Take out a journal or notebook and reflect on your earliest memories. Write down any significant events, experiences, or interactions from your childhood that come to mind. Focus on moments that have left an emotional impact, whether positive or negative. Consider the people involved, the feelings you experienced, and any patterns or themes that emerge.
Exploring Emotional Triggers	Think about situations or experiences in your adult life that trigger strong emotional responses. It could be feelings of anger, fear, sadness, or shame. Journal about these triggers, describing the circumstances and the emotions they evoke. Reflect on whether these emotional reactions might be connected to unresolved wounds from your childhood. Are there any similarities between the present situation and past experiences?
Identifying Patterns and Themes	Review your journal entries from Exercises 1 and 2. Look for recurring patterns or themes that emerge from your childhood memories and current emotional triggers. Do you notice commonalities in the types of experiences or relationships that evoke intense emotions? Consider how these patterns might relate to the wounds of your inner child.
Recognizing Unmet	Reflect on the emotional, physical, and psychological needs

Needs	that were not adequately met during your childhood. Consider whether there were moments when you felt ignored, invalidated, neglected, or unsupported. Write down any unmet needs that you identify and explore how they might have impacted your inner child's development and sense of self.
Examining Limiting Beliefs	Think about any negative or limiting beliefs you hold about yourself, others, or the world. These beliefs may include feelings of unworthiness, fear of abandonment, or a belief that you must always please others. Write down these beliefs and reflect on their origins. Consider how they may have been shaped by your childhood experiences and how they continue to affect your thoughts, behaviors, and relationships.
Connecting Emotions to Childhood Experiences	Choose one or two strong emotions that frequently arise for you in adulthood, such as anger, sadness, or anxiety. Explore the origins of these emotions by recalling specific childhood experiences that might have contributed to their development. Reflect on how these experiences have influenced your emotional landscape and how they continue to impact your present life.
Reflecting on Self-Healing	In this final exercise, consider what steps you can take to heal your inner child. Write down strategies and self-care practices that can support your healing journey. This may include seeking therapy, engaging in inner child work, practicing self-compassion, setting healthy boundaries, and nurturing your inner child's needs. Reflect on how committing to healing your inner child can positively impact your overall well-being and personal growth.

Completing these reflection exercises will provide you with a deeper understanding of your inner child's wounds and their origins. This newfound awareness serves as a foundation for initiating the healing process. Remember to approach this journey with self-compassion, patience, and the support of a therapist or counselor if needed. Healing the wounds of your inner child is a transformative and empowering path towards emotional well-being and a more authentic and fulfilling life.

Chapter 2: Reconnecting With The Inner Child

In this chapter, we will embark on the journey of reconnecting with our inner child—the wounded and vulnerable part of ourselves that holds the key to our healing and growth. By establishing a nurturing relationship with our inner child, we can create a safe and loving space for healing to take place.

2.1 Rebuilding The Connection With Your Inner Child

Rebuilding the connection with your inner child is a powerful and transformative process that involves nurturing, healing, and reconnecting with the younger version of yourself. It requires creating a safe and loving space within you to acknowledge, validate, and address the needs and wounds of your inner child. Here is a detailed explanation of how to rebuild the connection with your inner child:

One of the first steps in rebuilding the connection with your inner child is developing self-awareness. Take the time to observe and listen to your emotions, thoughts, and behaviors. Notice when you are triggered or experience strong emotional reactions, as these may be indicators of unresolved wounds from your childhood. By cultivating self-awareness, you can begin to recognize the presence and influence of your inner child in your daily life.

Next, practice self-compassion and self-acceptance. Approach your inner child with kindness, empathy, and unconditional love. Recognize that the experiences and emotions of your younger self are valid and deserving of compassion. Be patient with yourself as you navigate the healing process and offer reassurance and comfort to your inner child, assuring them that they are safe and supported.

Engage in inner child work and creative practices that allow for self-expression and connection. Explore activities that resonate with your inner child, such as drawing, writing, dancing, or playing. These activities tap into the playful and imaginative qualities of your inner child, facilitating a deeper connection and expression of your authentic self.

Another important aspect of rebuilding the connection with your inner child is re-parenting. This involves providing the care, support, and guidance that your inner child may have lacked during your childhood. Offer yourself nurturing and comforting gestures, such as wrapping yourself in a blanket, practicing self-soothing techniques, or engaging in self-care rituals. Develop a daily self-care routine that prioritizes your inner child's needs, allowing them to feel safe, loved, and nurtured.

Explore your inner child's unmet needs and work towards fulfilling them in healthy and empowering ways. Reflect on the specific needs that were not adequately met during your childhood, such as emotional validation, safety, or a sense of belonging. Seek opportunities to address these needs in your present life by seeking support from trusted friends, family, or therapists. Create healthy boundaries that protect your inner child and allow them to feel safe and secure.

Rebuilding the connection with your inner child also involves healing the wounds of the past. Engage in therapeutic techniques or seek the support of a qualified therapist who specializes in inner child work. This can help you process and release the emotional pain and trauma that may have been suppressed or ignored. Through therapy, you can gain valuable insights, develop coping mechanisms, and create a solid foundation for healing and growth.

Finally, practice forgiveness, both towards yourself and others. Recognize that your inner child may be holding onto resentment, anger, or hurt from past experiences. Release these negative emotions by forgiving yourself and those who may have caused pain. Forgiveness allows for healing and the restoration of inner peace, enabling you to move forward on your journey of reconnecting with your inner child.

Rebuilding the connection with your inner child is a lifelong process that requires commitment, self-compassion, and patience. As you nurture and heal your inner child, you will experience a deep sense of wholeness, authenticity, and emotional well-being. The reconnection with your inner child opens the door to personal growth, self-discovery, and a more vibrant and fulfilling life.

2.2 Creating A Safe Space For The Inner Child

Creating a safe space for the inner child is a crucial aspect of healing and reconnecting with the younger, vulnerable part of yourself. It involves establishing an environment, both internally and externally, where your inner child feels secure, accepted, and free to express their emotions and needs. Here is a detailed explanation of how to create a safe space for your inner child:

Cultivate self-awareness

Developing self-awareness is the foundation for creating a safe space for your inner child. Pay attention to your emotions, thoughts, and reactions throughout the day. Notice when you feel triggered or experience discomfort, as these are opportunities to understand and address the needs of your inner child.

Practice self-compassion and self-acceptance

Approach your inner child with kindness, understanding, and unconditional love. Recognize that the experiences and emotions of your younger self are valid and deserving of compassion. Be patient with yourself as you navigate the healing process, offering reassurance and comfort to your inner child.

Establish healthy boundaries

Set clear boundaries that protect your inner child and create a sense of safety. This includes saying no to situations or people that may trigger your inner child's wounds or compromise your well-being. Establishing boundaries allows you to create a protective space that fosters healing and growth.

Provide nurturing self-care

Engage in self-care practices that prioritize your inner child's needs. This can include activities such as taking relaxing baths, engaging in creative outlets, spending time in nature, or practicing mindfulness and meditation. Find ways to soothe and nurture yourself, offering the care and attention your inner child may have missed.

Validate and express emotions

Create a space where you can openly acknowledge and express your emotions. Allow yourself to feel without judgment or suppression. Validate your inner child's emotions by acknowledging their validity and importance. Journaling, talking to a trusted friend or therapist, or engaging in artistic expression can help you process and express your emotions in a safe and supportive way.

Engage in inner child work

Dedicate specific time for inner child work, where you intentionally connect with and nurture your inner child. This can involve visualization exercises, guided meditations, or journaling prompts that allow you to engage with the younger version of yourself and address their needs. Explore the interests, desires, and fears of your inner child, and validate their experiences.

Seek support

Surround yourself with a supportive network of friends, family, or therapists who understand and validate the importance of healing the inner child. Share your journey with trusted individuals who can provide a safe space for you to express your emotions and offer guidance and encouragement along the way.

Practice self-compassionate self-talk

Develop a nurturing and compassionate inner dialogue that supports your inner child. Replace self-criticism and negative self-talk with kind and encouraging words. Speak to yourself as you would to a beloved child, offering comfort, understanding, and encouragement.

Create a physical safe space

Designate a physical space, such as a cozy corner or a specific room, where you can retreat and connect with your inner child. Fill this space with items that evoke a sense of safety, comfort, and joy, such as stuffed animals, soft blankets, favorite books, or soothing music. This space serves as a tangible reminder of your commitment to nurturing your inner child.

Practice patience and consistency

Healing and creating a safe space for your inner child is a process that requires patience and consistency. Be gentle with yourself and understand that it may take time to fully establish a deep connection and trust with your inner child. Consistently engage in practices that support and nurture your inner child, even on days when it feels challenging.

2.3 Listening And Validating The Inner Child's Emotions

Listening to and validating the emotions of your inner child is a vital aspect of healing and reconnecting with this vulnerable part of yourself. It involves developing the ability to attune to and understand the emotions experienced by your inner child and providing them with the validation and support they may have missed during childhood. Here is a detailed explanation of how to listen to and validate the emotions of your inner child:

Cultivate awareness of emotions

Develop an awareness of the emotions that arise within you. Pay attention to the subtle shifts in your emotional landscape throughout the day. Notice when you experience feelings of joy, sadness, anger, fear, or any other emotions. Becoming attuned to your emotions is the first step in listening to and validating your inner child's emotions.

Practice active listening

When you notice emotions arising, create space to actively listen to them. Sit in a quiet and comfortable environment, and give yourself permission to fully experience and explore emotions. Avoid judgment or trying to change emotions. Instead, adopt an attitude of curiosity and openness, allowing the emotions to express themselves fully.

Engage in inner dialogue

Initiate a compassionate inner dialogue with your inner child. Acknowledge the emotions they are experiencing and validate their presence. Use kind and gentle language when talking to your inner child, offering reassurance that their emotions are valid and understandable.

Reflect on the origins of emotions

Explore the origins of the emotions you experience. Reflect on whether these emotions might be connected to past experiences or unmet needs from your childhood. Consider how these emotions may have influenced your beliefs, behaviors, and relationships. By understanding the root causes of your emotions, you can provide deeper validation and healing to your inner child.

Avoid suppressing or ignoring emotions

It is essential to create a safe space where you can express and process your emotions without judgment or suppression. Allow yourself to feel all emotions, even the ones that may be uncomfortable or painful. Suppressing or ignoring emotions can further isolate and wound your inner child. Validate and accept the full range of emotions that arise within you.

Provide self-compassion and comfort

When you notice your inner child experiencing intense emotions, offer yourself self-compassion and comfort. Speak to yourself with kindness and understanding, acknowledging the validity of your emotions. Use soothing and comforting gestures, such as gentle touch, self-hugging, or wrapping yourself in a cozy blanket. Provide the emotional support and nurturing that your inner child may have missed.

Validate without judgment

Practice validating your emotions without judgment. Recognize that all emotions are valid and serve a purpose. Avoid labeling emotions as good or bad, and instead, view them as signals from your inner child, indicating their needs and experiences. By validating your emotions without judgment, you create a safe space for your inner child to express themselves authentically.

Seek external validation

It can be beneficial to seek external validation from trusted individuals in your life. Share your emotions and experiences with friends, family, or a therapist who can offer a non-judgmental and empathetic listening ear. Hearing validation from others can reinforce the importance of acknowledging and honoring your emotions.

Engage in therapeutic practices

Consider engaging in therapeutic practices, such as journaling, art therapy, or somatic experiencing, to deepen your understanding and validation of your inner child's emotions. These practices provide additional avenues for expressing and processing emotions in a safe and supportive environment.

Practice patience and self-care

Healing and validating your inner child's emotions is an ongoing process that requires patience and self-care. Be gentle with yourself as you navigate the complexities of your emotions. Engage in regular self-care activities that nourish your emotional well-being and provide the space for your inner child to be heard and validated.

When you listen to and validate the emotions of your inner child, you are acknowledging their existence and honoring their experiences. This validation is crucial because, during childhood, your emotions may have been dismissed, ignored, or invalidated. As a result, your inner child may have learned to suppress or ignore their emotions, leading to unresolved emotional wounds.

By actively listening to your emotions and those of your inner child, you create a safe space for them to be expressed and heard. This process allows you to develop a deeper understanding of the underlying needs, fears and desires that drive your emotions. It also enables you to gain insights into the impact of past experiences on your emotional landscape.

Validating your inner child's emotions is an act of compassion and empathy. It involves recognizing the significance and legitimacy of their feelings without judgment or criticism. This validation communicates to your inner child that their emotions matter and are worthy of attention. It helps them feel seen, heard, and accepted, fostering a sense of safety and trust within themselves.

By validating your emotions, you break free from the cycle of self-judgment and self-criticism. Instead of dismissing or minimizing your emotions, you learn to honor and respect them. This shift in perspective allows you to develop a healthier relationship with your emotions, embracing them as valuable sources of information about your inner world.

When you validate your emotions, you can begin to identify patterns and themes that may have originated in childhood. Certain emotions may repeatedly arise in specific situations or relationships, signaling unresolved wounds or unmet needs. Recognizing these patterns enables you to address them directly, promoting healing and growth.

Validation of emotions also helps you develop emotional resilience. When you validate your inner child's emotions, you provide yourself with the opportunity to process and release pent-up emotional energy. This process contributes to a healthier emotional state, enabling you to navigate future challenges more effectively.

Furthermore, validation opens the door to self-compassion and self-care. When you validate your emotions, you cultivate a sense of kindness and understanding towards yourself. You learn to meet your own emotional needs and offer yourself the comfort, support, and nurturing that may have been lacking in the past.

Incorporating therapeutic practices into your journey of listening and validating emotions can be beneficial. Therapists or counselors trained in inner child work can provide guidance, support, and a safe space for exploring and validating your emotions. They can help you navigate any challenges or resistance that may arise during the process, facilitating deeper healing and integration.

2.4 Techniques For Nurturing Your Inner Child

Nurturing your inner child involves actively meeting their emotional, psychological, and physical needs. It is a process of providing the care, love, and support that may have been lacking during your childhood. Here are several techniques for nurturing your inner child in detail:

Inner Dialogue and Self-Talk

Engage in positive and nurturing inner dialogue with your inner child. Speak to yourself with kindness, compassion, and encouragement. Offer comforting words, reassurance, and validation. This technique helps to counteract negative self-talk and promotes a loving and supportive relationship with your inner child.

Imagery and Visualization

Use guided imagery and visualization techniques to connect with your inner child. Close your eyes, breathe deeply, and imagine yourself as a child. Visualize interacting with your younger self in a safe and nurturing environment. Engage in activities that your inner child enjoys, such as playing, exploring nature, or receiving love and care. This technique helps to establish a sense of safety and joy in your connection with your inner child.

Inner Child Journaling

Dedicate time for inner child journaling. Write a letter to your inner child expressing love, understanding, and support. Reflect on the experiences and emotions of your inner child and explore their needs and desires. Journaling provides an outlet for self-expression, self-reflection, and healing.

Creative Expression

Engage in creative activities that allow your inner child to express himself. Paint, draw, write stories or poems, dance, or play music. Embrace the freedom of creative expression and let your inner child's creativity flow. This technique taps into the imaginative and playful nature of your inner child, fostering self-discovery and emotional release.

Self-Care Rituals

Develop self-care rituals that prioritize your inner child's needs. Engage in activities that bring comfort and joy, such as taking baths, practicing mindfulness, cuddling with a soft blanket or stuffed animal, or engaging in hobbies that you enjoy. Create a routine of self-care that includes nurturing gestures specifically designed to meet your inner child's needs.

Reparenting Techniques

Reparenting involves providing the care and support that your inner child may have missed during childhood. Engage in reparenting techniques such as self-soothing, self-nurturing, and self-validation. Offer yourself the love, validation, and guidance that your inner child needs. Develop healthy boundaries that protect and nurture your inner child's well-being.

Inner Child Meditations

Practice guided meditations specifically designed to connect with and nurture your inner child. These meditations guide you through visualizations and affirmations that foster a sense of safety, love, and support for your inner child. Regular meditation helps to deepen your connection with your inner child and promotes inner healing.

Seeking Support

Reach out to supportive individuals, such as therapists, counselors, or support groups, who understand the importance of inner child healing. They can provide guidance, validation, and a safe space for you to explore and nurture your inner child. Seeking support from others who have also gone through similar healing journeys can be invaluable.

Inner Child Retreats or Workshops

Consider participating in inner child retreats or workshops facilitated by professionals trained in inner child work. These retreats provide a dedicated space and time for deep healing, nurturing, and reconnecting with your inner child. They offer opportunities for self-reflection, therapeutic exercises, and support from a community of like-minded individuals.

Patience and Self-Compassion

Nurturing your inner child is a process that requires patience, self-compassion, and consistency. Be gentle with yourself as you navigate the journey of healing and reconnecting. Understand that it takes time to build a strong relationship with your inner child and to heal the wounds of the past. Practice self-compassion and remind yourself that you are deserving of love, care, and nurturing.

Inner Dialogue and Self-Talk

Make a habit of regularly engaging in positive and nurturing self-talk. Speak to your inner child with love, kindness, and understanding. Offer words of encouragement, affirmation, and support. This practice helps to reframe negative beliefs and self-judgment, fostering a compassionate and nurturing inner environment.

Imagery and Visualization

Allow yourself to fully immerse yourself in the power of imagination and visualization. Create mental images or use pictures to evoke memories of your childhood. Visualize moments of joy, love, and safety, and re-experience those positive emotions. This technique helps to create a vivid connection with your inner child and facilitates healing and emotional release.

Inner Child Journaling

Set aside regular time for journaling specifically focused on your inner child. Write letters to your younger self, expressing empathy, compassion, and validation. Reflect on your childhood experiences, memories, and emotions. This practice allows for deeper self-reflection, insight, and understanding of your inner child's needs.

Creative Expression

Engage in creative activities that provide an outlet for your inner child's expression. Paint, draw, write, dance, or engage in any form of art that resonates with you. Embrace the freedom to play and explore creatively without judgment. Creative expression helps to bypass the analytical mind and allows your inner child to communicate and heal.

Self-Care Rituals

Develop self-care rituals that specifically cater to your inner child's needs. Create a routine that includes activities such as cuddling with a soft toy, taking bubble baths, engaging in playtime, or engaging in activities that bring you joy and comfort. These rituals send a powerful message to your inner child that their needs matter and deserve attention.

Reparenting Techniques

Reparenting involves consciously providing the care and support that your inner child may have missed during your childhood. Practice self-soothing by using a gentle touch, comforting gestures, or soothing self-talk. Nurture yourself through healthy routines, nutritious meals, and regular rest. Validate your emotions and offer yourself the love and acceptance that you may have longed for as a child.

Inner Child Meditations

Dedicate time to guided meditations specifically designed to connect with and nurture your inner child. These meditations often involve visualization, affirmations, and relaxation techniques that create a safe and loving space for your inner child to heal. Regular practice helps to strengthen the bond with your inner child and allows for deep emotional healing.

Seeking Support

Reach out to therapists, counselors, or support groups that specialize in inner child work. They can provide guidance, validation, and a safe space for you to explore and nurture your inner child. Sharing your experiences with others who understand and have similar healing journeys can provide a sense of validation, support, and connection.

Inner Child Retreats or Workshops

Consider attending retreats or workshops focused on inner child healing and nurturing. These dedicated spaces offer opportunities for immersive experiences, therapeutic exercises, and connection with others on a similar path. Retreats and workshops can provide a profound and transformative environment for deepening your inner child's healing journey.

Patience and Self-Compassion

Remember that nurturing your inner child is an ongoing process that requires patience, self-compassion, and consistency. Be patient with yourself as you navigate the ups and downs of healing. Offer yourself self-compassion and understanding during challenging moments.

Celebrate every small step you take towards nurturing and healing your inner child.

2.5 Workbook: Writing Exercises For Initiating A Dialogue With Your Inner Child

Here are some writing exercises you can use to initiate a dialogue with your inner child through a workbook:

Exercises	Explanation
Letter to Your Younger Self	Begin by writing a heartfelt letter to your younger self. Imagine you are speaking directly to the child version of yourself. Start by expressing love, compassion, and understanding. Acknowledge the challenges, pain, or difficult experiences your younger self may have faced. Apologize for any times you may have neglected or dismissed their needs. Share words of encouragement, validation, and reassurance. Write with authenticity and sincerity, allowing your inner child to feel seen, heard, and supported.
Journaling Prompts	Use specific journaling prompts to engage in a dialogue with your inner child. Some examples of prompts include: • "What was your favorite childhood memory, and why?" • "What were the challenges or struggles you faced as a child?" • "What were your dreams, hopes, and aspirations as a child?" • "What are the emotions that come up when you think about your childhood?" • "What are the needs and desires of your inner child that may still be unmet?" Allow your inner child to respond to these prompts through your writing.

	Write freely and without judgment, letting the words flow from your subconscious mind.
Inner Child Dialogue	Set up a dialogue on paper between your present self and your inner child. Start by writing a question or statement as your present self, and then allow your inner child to respond. Alternate between writing as your present self and your inner child. This technique helps to create a back-and-forth conversation, allowing you to explore your inner child's thoughts, feelings, and needs. It can also foster a deeper connection and understanding between your present self and your inner child.
Storytelling	Write a fictional story or narrative that represents the experiences and emotions of your inner child. Create characters and situations that reflect the challenges or dreams of your inner child. This exercise allows for a creative exploration of your inner child's world, enabling you to tap into their emotions and experiences in a more imaginative way. Write with curiosity and openness, allowing the story to unfold naturally.
Free Writing	Engage in a free writing exercise where you write continuously for a set period of time without censoring or editing your thoughts. Let your inner child guide the writing process. Write whatever comes to mind, allowing your inner child's voice to emerge. This technique encourages the subconscious mind to express itself freely and can reveal deeper insights into your inner child's thoughts and emotions.
Dialogue Completion	Start a dialogue with your inner child by writing a statement or question and leaving it incomplete. Then, allow your inner child to complete the dialogue by responding to the

	incomplete statement or question. This exercise can uncover hidden emotions or beliefs that your inner child may hold. It allows for a dynamic interaction between your present self and your inner child.
Visualization and Description	Visualize a specific memory from your childhood and describe it in detail. Engage your senses by vividly describing the sights, sounds, smells, tastes, and textures associated with that memory. Allow your inner child to guide the description, sharing their perspective and emotions. This exercise helps to bring your inner child's experiences to the surface, fostering a deeper connection and understanding.

These writing exercises are meant to facilitate a dialogue with your inner child and promote healing. Approach them with an open mind and heart, allowing your inner child to express themselves freely through your writing. The goal is to establish a compassionate and nurturing connection with your inner child, fostering healing and integration.

Chapter 3: Healing Childhood Wounds

In this chapter, we will delve into the process of healing childhood wounds—those deep emotional scars and traumas that have impacted our lives and shaped our beliefs and behaviors. By addressing these wounds, we can bring about profound healing, release emotional burdens, and create a foundation for a healthier and more fulfilling future.

3.1 Exploring And Understanding Childhood Wounds

Exploring and understanding childhood wounds is an essential step in the healing process. It involves delving into the experiences, events, and emotions from your childhood that have left lasting imprints and shaped your beliefs, behaviors, and relationships. Here is a detailed explanation of how to explore and understand childhood wounds:

Reflection and Self-Exploration

Take time for self-reflection and introspection. Create a safe and quiet space where you can explore your thoughts and emotions without judgment. Consider the significant events, relationships, and dynamics from your childhood. Reflect on how those experiences have influenced your beliefs, self-perception, and patterns of behavior.

Emotional Awareness

Develop an awareness of your emotions, both past and present. Identify and acknowledge the emotions that arise when you think about your childhood. These emotions can include pain, anger, sadness, fear, or even joy and love. Allow yourself to feel these emotions without judgment. Understanding and accepting your emotions is crucial for healing.

Triggers and Patterns

Pay attention to the triggers or situations that evoke strong emotional responses in your present life. Notice if there are any recurring patterns in your relationships or behaviors that stem from your childhood experiences. Recognizing these triggers and patterns can provide valuable insights into your unresolved childhood wounds.

Inner Child Work

Engage in inner child work to connect with your younger self and gain a deeper understanding of your childhood wounds. Visualize yourself as a child and listen to the needs, fears, and desires of that inner child. This process helps to establish empathy and compassion towards yourself and allows for a more profound exploration of your childhood wounds.

Seeking Perspective

Seek different perspectives on your childhood experiences. Talk to trusted friends, family members, or professionals who can offer insights and validate your experiences. They may provide alternative viewpoints or shed light on dynamics that were not apparent to you. Gathering different perspectives can help you gain a more comprehensive understanding of your childhood wounds.

Therapeutic Support

Consider working with a therapist or counselor experienced in trauma and childhood wounds. They can provide a safe and supportive environment for you to explore your past and navigate the emotions that arise. Therapeutic techniques such as trauma-focused therapy, inner child work, or cognitive-behavioral therapy can assist you in gaining a deeper understanding of your childhood wounds and developing effective coping strategies.

Journaling

Utilize journaling as a tool for self-reflection and exploration of your childhood wounds. Write about your memories, emotions, and thoughts related to your upbringing. Use prompts to delve deeper into specific aspects of your childhood experiences. Journaling allows for a private and introspective space to process and understand your wounds.

Compassion and Self-Forgiveness

Approach the exploration of your childhood wounds with compassion and self-forgiveness. Remember that you were a vulnerable child who may have experienced challenging circumstances. Practice self-compassion as you uncover painful memories and emotions. Forgive yourself for any perceived shortcomings or mistakes, recognizing that you did the best you could with the resources available to you at that time.

Integration and Healing

The purpose of exploring and understanding childhood wounds is to facilitate healing and integration. As you gain insights into your past, work on integrating those experiences into your present life. This process involves accepting the pain, releasing self-blame, and nurturing yourself with self-care, self-compassion, and self-love. Seek healing modalities that resonate with you, such as therapy, energy work, mindfulness practices, or support groups.

Core Beliefs

Childhood wounds often shape our core beliefs about ourselves, others, and the world. Take time to identify the core beliefs that have developed as a result of your childhood experiences. These beliefs may be negative or limiting, such as feeling unworthy, unlovable, or powerless. By recognizing these beliefs, you can begin to challenge and reframe them, allowing for healing and personal growth.

Patterns of Coping

Reflect on the coping mechanisms and defense mechanisms you developed as a child to navigate difficult situations or emotions. These patterns may have served you in the past but may no longer be beneficial in your adult life. Recognize any unhealthy patterns, such as avoidance, people-pleasing, or self-sabotage that may stem from your childhood wounds. Understanding these patterns can empower you to develop healthier coping strategies.

Impact on Relationships

Childhood wounds can significantly impact your relationships, both with yourself and others. Consider how your childhood experiences have influenced your ability to trust, form healthy attachments, and communicate effectively. Reflect on any patterns of behavior or dynamics that you notice in your relationships that may be linked to your childhood wounds. Understanding these patterns can help you develop healthier and more fulfilling relationships.

Inner Critic

Notice the presence of an inner critic or harsh self-judgment that may have developed as a result of childhood wounds. This critical voice often reinforces negative beliefs and can hinder your healing process. Become aware of the messages and judgments that arise within yourself, and work on cultivating self-compassion and self-acceptance. Recognize that the critical voice is not your true self but a product of your past experiences.

Validation and Healing of the Inner Child

As you explore your childhood wounds, it is essential to validate the emotions and experiences of your inner child. Allow yourself to grieve for any losses or pain that occurred during your childhood. Provide the nurturing and love that your inner child may have longed for. Engage in practices that help you connect with your inner child, such as visualization, journaling, or creative expression.

The Power of Forgiveness

Forgiveness plays a significant role in the healing process. This involves forgiving yourself for any perceived shortcomings or mistakes, as well as forgiving others who may have contributed to your childhood wounds. Forgiveness does not mean condoning or forgetting the past but rather freeing yourself from the burden of anger, resentment, and pain. It allows you to move forward with greater compassion and peace.

Integration and Growth

The ultimate goal of exploring and understanding childhood wounds is to integrate your past experiences into your present life and foster personal growth. As you gain insights and awareness, you can consciously make choices that align with your authentic self rather than being driven by unconscious wounds. Embrace opportunities for self-care, self-compassion, and self-growth. Engage in practices that nourish and empower you, such as mindfulness, self-reflection, and self-expression.

3.2 Processing And Releasing Emotional Pain

Processing and releasing emotional pain is a vital step in healing and moving forward from past traumas, wounds, and challenging experiences. Here is a detailed explanation of how to effectively process and release emotional pain:

Acknowledge and Validate

The first step in processing emotional pain is to acknowledge its presence and validate your feelings. Recognize that it is normal to experience a range of emotions, including sadness, anger, fear, or grief, in response to painful experiences. Avoid judging or suppressing your emotions. Instead, create a safe space for yourself to express and validate your feelings without judgment.

Self-Reflection and Awareness

Engage in self-reflection to gain a deeper understanding of the emotional pain you are experiencing. Explore the underlying causes, triggers, and patterns associated with your pain. Pay attention to any recurring thoughts, beliefs, or memories that intensify your emotional distress. Increased self-awareness can help you identify the root causes of your pain and guide your healing process.

Emotional Release Techniques

Find healthy and constructive ways to release your emotions. These techniques may include:

- **Journaling:** Write freely about your emotions, thoughts, and experiences. Allow your emotions to flow onto the pages without censorship. This process can provide a sense of release, clarity, and insight.

- **Artistic Expression:** Engage in creative outlets such as painting, drawing, sculpting, or dancing. Express your emotions through artistic mediums, allowing the creative process to facilitate emotional release.

- **Physical Exercise:** Engaging in physical activities like running, dancing, or yoga can help release pent-up emotions and promote the production of endorphins, which can improve mood and alleviate pain.

- **Mindfulness and Meditation:** Practice mindfulness and meditation to cultivate a non-judgmental awareness of your emotions. This allows you to observe your pain without becoming overwhelmed by it. Mindfulness and meditation can also create space for self-compassion and self-soothing.

- **Breathwork:** Utilize breathing techniques to calm your nervous system and release emotional tension. Deep belly breathing, box breathing, or alternate nostril breathing can help you relax and let go of emotional pain.

- **Somatic Practices:** Explore somatic practices such as body scanning, body awareness exercises, or yoga to connect with the sensations and emotions held in your body. Pay attention to areas of tension or discomfort, allowing yourself to release and process emotional pain on a physical level.

Seeking Support

Reach out for support from trusted friends, family members, or professionals. Consider therapy or counseling as a way to process and release emotional pain in a safe and supportive environment. A trained therapist can guide you through the healing process, provide tools and techniques for emotional release, and offer a compassionate space to explore and heal.

Self-Compassion and Self-Care

Practice self-compassion and self-care as you navigate emotional pain. Treat yourself with kindness, understanding, and patience. Engage in activities that bring you joy, relaxation, and comfort. Prioritize self-care practices such as getting enough sleep, eating nourishing foods, and engaging in activities that support your well-being.

Rituals and Ceremonies

Consider incorporating rituals or ceremonies into your healing process. These can be personal and meaningful to you. They may involve lighting candles, writing letters for release, creating an altar, or performing a symbolic gesture to signify letting go of emotional pain. Rituals can provide closure and a sense of empowerment.

Forgiveness

Explore the concept of forgiveness as a way to release emotional pain. Forgiveness does not mean condoning or forgetting what happened. It is a process of releasing the resentment, anger, and desire for revenge that may be tied to emotional pain. Forgiveness is a personal choice that can bring inner peace and liberation from emotional burdens.

Patience and Time

Healing emotional pain takes time, and everyone's journey is unique. Be patient with yourself as you process and release your pain. Allow yourself to experience the full range of emotions without rushing the healing process. Give yourself permission to heal at your own pace and celebrate the progress you make along the way.

Emotional Catharsis

Emotional catharsis involves allowing yourself to fully experience and express your emotions. It can be helpful to find a private and safe space where you can let your emotions flow freely. This may involve crying, screaming into a pillow, or engaging in any form of expressive release that feels authentic to you. Emotional catharsis can provide a sense of relief and release pent-up emotions.

Inner Child Healing

Emotional pain often stems from unresolved wounds from childhood. By focusing on healing your inner child, you can address the core emotional pain that may be deeply ingrained. Connect with your inner child through visualization, meditation, or inner child therapy techniques. Offer comfort, love, and reassurance to your inner child, providing the emotional nurturing they may have lacked in the past.

Embracing Vulnerability

Processing and releasing emotional pain requires a willingness to be vulnerable. It involves allowing yourself to be open, honest, and raw with your emotions. Embrace vulnerability by sharing your feelings with trusted individuals, such as close friends, family members, or a therapist. Vulnerability allows for deeper emotional connections and can facilitate healing.

Gratitude and Positive Focus

While it is essential to acknowledge and process emotional pain, it is also important to cultivate a positive mindset. Practice gratitude by focusing on the aspects of your life that bring you joy, love, and happiness. Engage in activities that promote positive emotions and self-care. By shifting your focus to the positive aspects of your life, you can counterbalance the weight of emotional pain.

Letting Go

Releasing emotional pain involves actively letting go of what no longer serves you. This may involve forgiveness, both for yourself and others involved in the pain. Understand that holding onto resentment and anger only prolongs the pain. Letting go is a choice that empowers you to move forward and create space for healing and growth.

Professional Support

If the emotional pain feels overwhelming or persistent, consider seeking professional support. A therapist or counselor can provide guidance, tools, and techniques specific to your needs. They can assist you in navigating the depths of your emotions, facilitate healing, and provide a safe space for processing and releasing emotional pain.

Integration and Self-Reflection

As you process and release emotional pain, take time to integrate the lessons and insights gained from your experiences. Engage in self-reflection to understand how your past pain has shaped you and identify the changes you want to make moving forward. Embrace the opportunity for personal growth and commit to making choices that align with your healed and empowered self.

3.3 Techniques For Healing Childhood Wounds

Healing childhood wounds is a transformative and often ongoing process that involves addressing and resolving the emotional pain and trauma that originated in early life experiences. Here are some techniques that can be helpful in healing childhood wounds:

Therapeutic Support

Seeking professional help from a therapist or counselor trained in trauma and childhood wounds is a crucial step in the healing process. They can provide a safe and supportive environment where you can explore and process your emotions, gain insights into your experiences, and develop coping strategies. Therapists may use various modalities, such as cognitive-behavioral therapy (CBT), dialectical behavior therapy (DBT), eye movement desensitization and reprocessing (EMDR), or somatic experiencing, tailored to your specific needs.

Inner Child Work

Inner child work involves connecting with and healing your wounded inner child. It can be done through visualization, guided meditation, or inner child therapy techniques. By nurturing and comforting your inner child, you can address unmet needs, provide the love and support that may have been lacking in your childhood, and build a healthier relationship with yourself.

Emotional Regulation Techniques

Childhood wounds often result in emotional dysregulation. Learning and practicing emotional regulation techniques can help you manage overwhelming emotions and create a sense of stability and control. These techniques may include deep breathing exercises, grounding techniques, mindfulness meditation, and progressive muscle relaxation. Developing emotional regulation, skills can provide a foundation for healing and reduce the impact of triggers related to childhood wounds.

Expressive Arts Therapy

Engaging in expressive arts therapy can be a powerful tool for healing childhood wounds. This therapy involves using creative outlets such as painting, drawing, writing, or music to express emotions and explore the impact of childhood experiences. Through artistic expression, you can tap into unconscious feelings, release emotional pain, and gain insights and clarity about your wounds.

Journaling

Writing in a journal can be a cathartic and introspective practice for healing childhood wounds. Set aside regular time to reflect on your experiences, emotions, and thoughts related to your childhood. Write freely and without judgment, allowing your feelings and memories to flow onto the pages. Journaling can help you gain a deeper understanding of your wounds, identify patterns, and track your progress over time.

Self-Compassion and Self-Care

Cultivating self-compassion and engaging in self-care practices are essential components of healing childhood wounds. Treat yourself with kindness, understanding, and patience as you navigate the healing process. Practice self-care activities that promote your well-being, such as engaging in hobbies, spending time in nature, practicing mindfulness, setting boundaries, and seeking moments of relaxation and joy.

Prioritizing self-care supports your overall healing and fosters a nurturing relationship with yourself.

Boundaries and Assertiveness

Healing childhood wounds often involves developing healthy boundaries and assertiveness skills. Learn to identify and set boundaries to protect yourself from further harm and create a sense of safety. Practice assertiveness by expressing your needs, desires, and emotions in a clear and respectful manner. Building healthy boundaries and assertiveness skills empowers you to advocate for yourself and establish healthier relationships.

Supportive Relationships

Surrounding yourself with supportive and understanding individuals is crucial in the healing process. Seek out relationships with friends, family members, or support groups who can provide empathy, validation, and a safe space to share your experiences. Connecting with others who have similar experiences can offer a sense of belonging and validation, reinforcing that you are not alone in your healing journey.

Mind-Body Practices

Engaging in mind-body practices, such as yoga, tai chi, or qigong, can be beneficial for healing childhood wounds. These practices promote the integration of the mind and body, help release stored emotional tension, and cultivate a sense of calm and self-awareness. By connecting with your body and its sensations, you can develop a deeper understanding of how childhood wounds have impacted you physically and emotionally.

Forgiveness and Letting Go

Forgiveness is a complex and personal process that can support healing childhood wounds. It involves letting go of resentment and anger towards those who may have caused you harm. Forgiveness does not mean forgetting or condoning the actions but rather releasing the emotional burden and freeing yourself from the pain associated with the past. Remember, forgiveness is a journey, and it may require time and self-reflection.

EMDR (Eye Movement Desensitization and Reprocessing)

EMDR is a therapeutic technique specifically designed to help individuals process and heal from traumatic experiences, including childhood wounds. It involves bilateral stimulation of the brain, such as eye movements, hand tapping, or auditory tones, while focusing on traumatic memories or distressing emotions. EMDR helps reprocess traumatic memories, reduces their emotional intensity, and promotes healing and resolution.

Reparenting and Self-Nurturing

Reparenting is a technique that involves providing yourself with the love, care, and nurturing that you may have missed during childhood. You can engage in activities that symbolize nurturing, such as wrapping yourself in a soft blanket, giving yourself positive affirmations, or engaging in self-soothing behaviors. Reparenting helps meet your emotional needs, develop self-compassion, and foster a sense of safety and security.

Inner Dialogue and Self-Reflection

Engaging in an inner dialogue with your inner child can facilitate healing. Take time to have a conversation with your inner child, listening to their needs, fears, and desires. Write letters or journal entries from the perspective of your inner child, allowing them to express themselves freely. This process can foster understanding, empathy, and connection and provide an opportunity to address and heal the wounds that still affect you.

Trauma-Informed Yoga

Trauma-informed yoga incorporates gentle movement, breathwork, and mindfulness practices to promote healing from trauma, including childhood wounds. This type of yoga emphasizes creating a safe and supportive environment, offering choices and autonomy in movements, and focusing on present-moment experiences. Trauma-informed yoga can help release tension held in the body, regulate the nervous system, and cultivate a sense of grounding and empowerment.

Revisiting and Reframing Memories

As part of the healing process, you may choose to revisit and reframe your childhood memories. This can involve viewing past experiences from a different perspective, seeking out additional information or context, or challenging negative beliefs that stem from those memories. Reframing memories can provide a new understanding, reduce the emotional charge associated with the events, and foster healing and growth.

Rituals and Ceremonies

Engaging in rituals or ceremonies can be a powerful way to honor and release childhood wounds. These can be personal and meaningful to you. For example, you might create a ritual where you write down the painful experiences on pieces of paper and then burn them as a symbol of releasing their hold on you. Rituals and ceremonies provide a sense of closure, allowing you to let go of the past and embrace your healing journey.

Energy Healing Modalities

Various energy healing modalities, such as Reiki, acupuncture, or sound therapy, can support the healing of childhood wounds. These modalities work with the body's energy system to restore balance, release emotional blockages, and promote healing. They can be used alongside other therapeutic techniques to enhance the healing process and create a harmonious mind-body connection.

Creating a Supportive Inner Circle

Surrounding yourself with a supportive and understanding inner circle can greatly aid in healing childhood wounds. Seek out relationships with individuals who are empathetic, validating, and nurturing. Share your experiences with them, and allow yourself to receive their support and encouragement. Having a supportive network can provide a sense of safety, validation, and belonging as you navigate the healing journey.

3.4 Forgiveness And Compassion Towards Yourself And Others

Forgiveness and compassion are transformative practices that can facilitate healing and promote emotional well-being. When applied to oneself and others, they have the power to release resentment, anger, and pain, allowing for growth, understanding, and inner peace. Here's a detailed explanation of forgiveness and compassion:

Forgiveness Towards Yourself

Self-forgiveness involves letting go of self-blame, guilt, and harsh judgment for past mistakes, regrets, or shortcomings. It is acknowledging that you are human, fallible, and deserving of compassion and understanding. Self-forgiveness does not mean condoning harmful actions or denying responsibility; rather, it is about acknowledging the past, learning from it, and choosing to move forward with kindness towards yourself.

- Reflection and Acceptance: Take time to reflect on your actions, choices, and behaviors that have caused harm or pain to yourself or others. Accept the reality of what has happened without judgment or self-condemnation. Recognize that mistakes are opportunities for growth and learning.

- Compassion and Understanding: Cultivate self-compassion by offering yourself the same kindness and understanding you would extend to a close friend. Recognize that you were doing the best you could at the time, given your circumstances, knowledge, and resources. Embrace your humanity and inherent worthiness of love and forgiveness.

- Learning and Growth: Use the experience as an opportunity for growth and personal development. Identify the lessons learned and how you can make amends or change your behavior moving forward. Commit to self-improvement and making choices aligned with your values and the person you aspire to be.

- Releasing the Emotional Burden: Forgiving yourself involves releasing the emotional burden and freeing yourself from the negative emotions associated with past actions or decisions. It allows you to heal, move forward, and create a more positive and compassionate relationship with yourself.

Forgiveness Towards Others

Forgiving others is a process of letting go of resentment, anger, and the desire for revenge or punishment. It is not about condoning or forgetting the actions that caused harm; instead, it is a personal choice to release the emotional burden and find inner peace.

- Understanding and Empathy: Seek to understand the motivations, experiences, and circumstances that may have led someone to hurt or harm you. Cultivate empathy by putting yourself in their shoes and recognizing that people are fallible and often act from their own wounds and limitations.

- Compassion and Detachment: Practice compassion by recognizing the shared human experience of suffering and imperfection. Understand that holding onto resentment only perpetuates your own pain and hinders your healing. Detach yourself from the need for revenge or retribution and choose compassion instead.

- Boundaries and Self-Protection: Forgiveness does not mean allowing harmful behavior to continue. Set clear boundaries to protect yourself from further harm and establish healthy dynamics in your relationships. Forgiveness can coexist with the choice to distance yourself from toxic or abusive individuals.

- Emotional Release and Healing: Forgiveness frees you from the burden of carrying negative emotions toward others. It allows you to release the emotional pain, resentment, and anger, fostering your own emotional well-being and inner peace.

Compassion Towards Yourself and Others

Compassion is an attitude of kindness, understanding, and empathy towards oneself and others. It involves recognizing the shared human experience of suffering and responding with a gentle and caring approach.

- Self-Compassion: Treat yourself with kindness, understanding, and patience in times of difficulty or pain. Be supportive and nurturing towards yourself, especially during challenging moments. Offer yourself words of comfort, engage in self-care practices, and embrace self-acceptance and self-love.

- Empathy and Understanding: Extend empathy and understanding towards others, recognizing that they, too, experience their own challenges, struggles, and wounds. Practice active listening, seeking to understand their perspective, and respond with kindness and compassion.

- Letting Go of Resentment: Cultivate a mindset of letting go and moving forward, releasing grudges and resentments towards yourself and others. Holding onto anger and resentment only perpetuates suffering and hinders personal growth and healing.

- Cultivating Connection and Healing: Compassion fosters connection and healing, both within oneself and in relationships with others. By approaching yourself and others with kindness and empathy, you create a supportive and nurturing environment for growth, understanding, and healing.

Self-Compassion in Action

Self-compassion involves treating yourself with the same care and kindness you would offer to a loved one in need. It means recognizing your own suffering and responding with empathy and understanding. Here are some practical ways to cultivate self-compassion:

- Self-Care Practices: Engage in activities that nourish and replenish your physical, emotional, and mental well-being. This may include practicing mindfulness, taking breaks when needed, engaging in hobbies you enjoy, or seeking professional help when necessary.

- Positive Self-Talk: Monitor your internal dialogue and replace self-critical thoughts with supportive and compassionate statements. Offer yourself words of encouragement and understanding, focusing on your strengths and resilience.

- Self-Forgiveness Rituals: Create rituals or practices that symbolize self-forgiveness. This can involve writing a forgiveness letter to yourself, engaging in self-forgiveness meditation, or using visualization techniques to imagine letting go of self-blame and embracing self-compassion.

Cultivating Empathy and Understanding

Compassion towards others involves cultivating empathy and understanding of their experiences and struggles. Here's how you can deepen your capacity for empathy:

- Active Listening: Practice active listening when engaging in conversations with others. Truly listen to their words, tone, and non-verbal cues. Seek to understand their perspective without judgment or interruption.

- Perspective-Taking: Put yourself in the shoes of others to gain a better understanding of their experiences. Imagine what it might be like to walk their path, considering their background, challenges, and emotions.

- Challenging Assumptions: Recognize that everyone has their own unique story and motivations. Challenge assumptions or preconceived notions you may have about others, allowing space for a more compassionate and open-minded perspective.

- Practice Forgiveness in Small Ways: Practice forgiving others for minor offenses or grievances. This can help you develop a mindset of forgiveness and openness, making it easier to extend forgiveness in more significant situations.

Gratitude and Appreciation

Cultivating gratitude can enhance compassion and forgiveness towards yourself and others. Focus on the positive aspects of your life and acknowledge the good in others. Expressing gratitude can shift your perspective, foster a sense of interconnectedness, and create a more compassionate mindset.

Self-Reflection and Personal Growth

Engage in self-reflection to gain insights into your own behavior, patterns, and triggers. This self-awareness allows you to identify areas for personal growth and take proactive steps toward healing and self-improvement.

- Learning from Mistakes: Instead of dwelling on past mistakes, view them as opportunities for growth and learning. Reflect on the lessons you have gained from those experiences, which can help prevent repeating similar patterns in the future.

- Making Amends: If appropriate and possible, consider making amends to those you may have hurt or harmed in the past. This can be a powerful step towards healing and reconciliation, fostering forgiveness from both parties involved.

- Seeking Professional Support: In some cases, childhood wounds or past experiences may be deeply ingrained and challenging to address alone. Seeking support from a therapist or counselor can provide guidance, tools, and a safe space to navigate the healing process.

3.5 Workbook: Guided Exercises For Healing Specific Childhood Wounds

A workbook with guided exercises for healing specific childhood wounds can be a valuable tool in the healing process. These exercises provide structured and focused activities to explore and address specific areas of childhood wounds. Here is a

detailed explanation of how such a workbook can assist in healing:

Exercises	Explanation
Identifying Specific Childhood Wounds	The workbook begins by helping you identify and acknowledge the specific childhood wounds that have had a lasting impact on your life. It may prompt you to reflect on different aspects such as emotional, physical, or psychological wounds, neglect, abandonment, or trauma. By recognizing these wounds, you create a foundation for the healing journey.
Providing Guided Reflection	The workbook offers guided reflection exercises that encourage you to delve deeper into specific childhood wounds. It may prompt you to explore the emotions, beliefs, and patterns associated with each wound. The exercises might involve journaling, writing letters to your younger self, or engaging in artistic expressions to foster self-expression and self-awareness.

Healing Strategies and Techniques	The workbook introduces a range of healing strategies and techniques tailored to address specific childhood wounds. It may provide instructions for practices such as mindfulness meditation, visualization, breathwork, or somatic exercises to release stored emotions and promote healing. These techniques are designed to help you process and integrate the pain associated with childhood wounds.
Reconstructing Healthy Beliefs and Patterns	The workbook guides you through exercises to challenge and reframe negative beliefs and patterns that have emerged from childhood wounds. It may include activities to identify and replace self-limiting beliefs with empowering and affirming ones. By reconstructing healthier beliefs and patterns, you can cultivate a more positive self-image and build healthier relationships.
Inner Child Healing	The workbook may include exercises specifically focused on healing the inner child. These exercises provide a safe space for you to nurture, validate, and connect with your inner child. They may involve guided visualizations, dialogue, or role-playing techniques to facilitate healing and foster a sense of self-compassion and self-acceptance.
Integration and Transformation	The workbook helps you integrate the healing work into your daily life. It may include exercises to develop self-care practices, establish healthy boundaries, and foster self-compassion. By incorporating these practices, you support ongoing healing and transformation, allowing the lessons and insights gained from the exercises to manifest in your day-to-day experiences.
Progress Tracking and Reflection	The workbook encourages you to track your progress and reflect on the changes and growth you have experienced throughout the healing journey. It may include space for journaling, recording insights, and noting positive shifts in thoughts, emotions, and behaviors. Regularly revisiting

	these reflections can provide motivation and reinforce the progress made.
Support and Resources	The workbook may provide additional resources such as recommended readings, supportive online communities, or suggestions for seeking professional help when needed. These resources offer ongoing support and guidance throughout the healing process.

Chapter 4: Reparenting The Inner Child

In this chapter, we will explore the concept of reparenting the inner child—a vital process in healing and nurturing the wounded aspects of ourselves. By becoming the loving and supportive parent that our inner child needs, we can provide the care, validation, and guidance that may have been missing during our formative years.

4.1 Becoming Your Own Loving Parent

"Becoming your own loving parent" is a concept rooted in inner child work and self-compassion. It involves developing a nurturing and supportive relationship with yourself, where you take on the role of a loving and caring parent to your own inner child. This process can help heal childhood wounds, promote self-acceptance, and cultivate emotional well-being. Here's a detailed explanation of how to become your own loving parent:

Self-Reflection and Understanding

Begin by reflecting on your childhood experiences and the parenting you received. Identify any patterns, beliefs, or behaviors that may have resulted from those experiences. This self-reflection allows you to gain insight into the ways you may have internalized negative or critical messages from your upbringing.

Recognizing the Inner Child

Develop an awareness of your inner child, which represents your vulnerable and authentic self. Acknowledge that the inner child holds your emotions, needs, and desires. By recognizing this inner child within you, you can begin to understand and address their wounds and provide the care and love they may have lacked in the past.

Cultivating Self-Compassion

Practice self-compassion by treating yourself with kindness, understanding, and acceptance. Offer yourself the same care, empathy, and support you would give to a beloved child. Embrace your imperfections, acknowledge your emotions, and respond to yourself with compassion rather than judgment or self-criticism.

Meeting Emotional Needs

Become attuned to your emotional needs and provide yourself with the nurturing and support you require. This includes validating your feelings, giving yourself permission to experience and express emotions, and offering comfort and reassurance during challenging times. Ask yourself what you need in moments of distress and respond with love and care.

Establishing Healthy Boundaries

Set healthy boundaries to protect and nurture yourself. Learn to recognize and respect your own limits and communicate them assertively. This involves saying "no" when necessary, prioritizing self-care, and creating an environment that fosters your emotional well-being.

Positive Self-Talk and Affirmations

Develop a practice of positive self-talk and affirmations. Replace self-critical or negative thoughts with loving and affirming messages. Speak to yourself with kindness and encouragement, reminding yourself of your worth, strengths, and potential.

Engaging in Self-Care

Prioritize self-care activities that promote your overall well-being. This includes engaging in activities that bring you joy, practicing relaxation techniques, nurturing your physical health, and pursuing hobbies and interests that fulfill you. By prioritizing self-care, you demonstrate love and care for your own well-being.

Inner Child Healing

Engage in inner child healing practices to connect with and heal your inner child. This can involve visualization exercises, journaling, or engaging in playful activities that evoke a sense of joy and spontaneity. By nurturing and healing your inner child, you provide them with love and care they may have missed in their formative years.

Seeking Support

If needed, seek support from a therapist or counselor who specializes in inner child work or trauma. A professional can guide you through the healing process, provide additional tools and techniques, and offer a safe space for exploration and growth.

Practice, Patience, and Persistence

Becoming your own loving parent is a process that requires practice, patience, and persistence. It involves consistently showing up for yourself with love, compassion, and understanding. Over time, this practice can transform your relationship with yourself and foster deep healing and emotional well-being.

Reparenting the Inner Child

Reparenting refers to the process of providing the care and nurturing that your inner child may have missed during your upbringing. It involves stepping into the role of a loving, supportive, and reliable caregiver to yourself. This may include offering comfort during times of distress, setting healthy boundaries, providing encouragement and validation, and meeting your own emotional needs.

Healing the Parent-Child Dynamic

Becoming your own loving parent allows you to heal the wounds associated with the parent-child dynamic. By developing a compassionate and nurturing relationship with yourself, you can address any unresolved issues from your past and create a new internal narrative that promotes self-love and self-acceptance.

Overcoming Self-Defeating Patterns

As you become your own loving parent, you can identify and overcome self-defeating patterns and behaviors that may have been ingrained during childhood. By providing yourself with love, guidance, and encouragement, you can challenge and transform negative self-beliefs and behaviors, fostering personal growth and empowerment.

Inner Alignment and Integration

Becoming your own loving parent helps you cultivate inner alignment and integration. It involves bridging the gap between your adult self and your wounded inner child, allowing them to coexist in a balanced and harmonious way. This integration enables you to make decisions and choices that align with your values, needs, and desires while acknowledging and honoring the emotions and experiences of your inner child.

Breaking the Cycle

Becoming your own loving parent can break the cycle of generational patterns and trauma. By consciously nurturing and caring for yourself, you can create a different experience for future generations. This process allows you to provide a positive model of self-love, self-compassion, and healthy relationships, contributing to the healing of your family lineage.

Embracing Vulnerability and Authenticity

Becoming your own loving parent requires embracing vulnerability and authenticity. It means allowing yourself to be seen and heard, acknowledging and honoring your true emotions, and expressing yourself authentically. By embracing vulnerability, you create an environment of self-acceptance and self-love, fostering a deeper connection with yourself and others.

Cultivating Resilience and Inner Strength

Through the practice of becoming your own loving parent, you cultivate resilience and inner strength. By providing yourself with the support, encouragement, and care you need, you develop a strong foundation from which to navigate life's challenges. This resilience empowers you to face adversity with compassion, self-assurance, and a greater sense of self-worth.

Creating Loving Relationships

Becoming your own loving parent enhances your ability to create loving and healthy relationships with others. As you learn to provide love, acceptance, and support to yourself, you become better equipped to offer the same qualities to others. This fosters deeper connections, empathy, and understanding in your interactions with loved ones and creates a positive ripple effect in your relationships.

4.2 Providing The Care And Support Your Inner Child Needs

Providing the care and support your inner child needs is a crucial aspect of inner child healing and self-nurturing. It involves creating a nurturing environment within yourself where you can address the unmet needs and emotional wounds of your inner child. Here's a detailed explanation of how to provide care and support for your inner child:

Recognition and Awareness

Begin by recognizing the presence of your inner child within you. Acknowledge that this inner child represents your authentic self, holding your emotions, needs, and vulnerabilities. Develop an awareness of when your inner child is activated, such as when you experience intense emotions or react in ways that are reminiscent of your childhood.

Attunement and Validation

Tune into the emotions and needs of your inner child. Pay attention to the feelings that arise within you and validate them. Acknowledge that your emotions are valid and worthy of attention and care. Offer comfort and reassurance to your inner child, letting them know that their emotions matter and that they are safe to express themselves.

Active Listening

Practice active listening to your inner child's needs. Take time to listen deeply to the messages and desires that arise from within you. Engage in self-reflection and introspection to understand what your inner child is longing for. By giving your inner child a voice and genuinely listening to their needs, you can begin to meet them with compassion and understanding.

Compassionate Self-Talk

Engage in compassionate self-talk when addressing your inner child's needs. Replace self-criticism and negative self-talk with kind, loving, and supportive inner dialogue. Offer words of encouragement, understanding, and comfort to your inner child. Speak to yourself as you would to a beloved child, providing the nurturing and soothing words they need to hear.

Emotional Expression

Create a safe space for your inner child to express their emotions. Allow yourself to feel and express a wide range of emotions without judgment or suppression. Engage in activities that facilitate emotional expression, such as journaling, artwork, or talking with a trusted friend. By honoring and expressing your emotions, you validate and acknowledge your inner child's emotional needs.

Revisiting Past Experiences

Take time to revisit past experiences and memories that may have caused pain or wounded your inner child. Approach these memories with self-compassion and curiosity. Reflect on how those experiences have shaped your beliefs, behaviors, and emotions. Through this process, you can gain a deeper understanding of your inner child's wounds and develop empathy toward yourself.

Reparenting and Self-Care

Reparent your inner child by providing the care and support they need. Engage in self-care practices that nourish your physical, emotional, and mental well-being. This may involve activities such as taking soothing baths, practicing mindfulness, engaging in hobbies that bring you joy, or seeking professional support when necessary. Prioritize self-care as an act of love and care for your inner child.

Setting Boundaries

Establish healthy boundaries to protect and nurture your inner child. Learn to recognize and honor your limits in relationships, work, and other aspects of life. Communicate your boundaries assertively and assert your right to be treated with respect and dignity. Setting boundaries ensures that your inner child feels safe and protected.

Seeking Support

If necessary, seek support from a therapist or counselor who specializes in inner child work or trauma. A professional can provide guidance, tools, and a safe space for exploring and healing your inner child's wounds. They can help you navigate the healing process and offer insights and perspectives that facilitate growth and transformation.

Consistency and Patience

Providing care and support for your inner child is an ongoing process that requires consistency and patience. Be patient with yourself as you navigate the healing journey. Cultivate a compassionate attitude towards your inner child and embrace the understanding that healing takes time and effort.

4.3 Setting Healthy Boundaries And Nurturing Self-Care Practices

Setting healthy boundaries and nurturing self-care practices are essential components of self-care and maintaining emotional well-being. Here's a detailed explanation of each:

Define Your Limits

Take the time to identify what is acceptable and what is not in your relationships and interactions. Consider your emotional, physical, and mental limits and establish boundaries that honor and protect them.

- Communicate Assertively: Clearly and respectfully communicate your boundaries to others. Express your needs and expectations, and assert your right to be treated with respect and dignity. Practice effective communication skills to ensure that your boundaries are understood and respected.

- Say No Without Guilt: Learn to say "no" when something goes against your boundaries or does not align with your values or well-being. Set boundaries around your time, energy, and resources, and prioritize self-care without feeling guilty or obligated to please others.

- Protect Yourself: Boundaries act as protective barriers, safeguarding your emotional and mental well-being. They help prevent emotional exhaustion, burnout, and resentment by creating space for self-care and maintaining healthy relationships.

- Adjust as Needed: Boundaries are not set in stone; they can be adjusted based on your evolving needs and circumstances. Regularly assess your boundaries and make adjustments to ensure they continue to serve your well-being.

Nurturing Self-Care Practices

Self-care practices involve intentionally engaging in activities that promote your physical, mental, and emotional well-being. These practices are essential for maintaining balance, reducing stress, and replenishing your energy. When you prioritize self-care, you:

- Identify Your Needs: Take the time to identify your physical, emotional, and mental needs. Consider what brings you joy, relaxation, and a sense of fulfillment. This awareness helps you tailor your self-care practices to suit your unique needs.

- Create a Routine: Incorporate self-care activities into your daily or weekly routine. Set aside dedicated time for self-care, and make it a non-negotiable part of your schedule. Treat self-care as a priority rather than an afterthought.

- Engage in Activities You Enjoy: Engage in activities that bring you pleasure and nourishment. It could be hobbies, exercise, spending time in nature, reading, practicing mindfulness, or engaging in creative pursuits. Choose activities that resonate with you and help you recharge.

- Practice Mindfulness and Relaxation: Cultivate mindfulness and relaxation techniques as part of your self-care routine. This may include meditation, deep breathing exercises, yoga, or engaging in activities that promote relaxation and stress reduction.

- Prioritize Physical Well-being: Take care of your physical health by getting adequate sleep, nourishing your body with nutritious food, and engaging in regular exercise. Pay attention to your body's signals and provide it with the care and attention it needs.

- Emotional Well-being: Prioritize your emotional well-being by engaging in activities that support emotional balance and self-reflection. This may involve journaling, therapy or counseling, connecting with loved ones, or seeking support when needed.

- Set Healthy Digital Boundaries: Establish boundaries around your use of technology and digital devices. Set aside designated periods of time for digital detox and limit exposure to screens when it is necessary for your well-being.

- Practice Self-Compassion: Approach self-care with a mindset of self-compassion and non-judgment. Be kind and gentle with yourself, and let go of any self-imposed pressure to be perfect. Embrace self-care as a loving act towards yourself.

4.4 Cultivating Self-Compassion And Self-Love

Cultivating self-compassion and self-love is a transformative practice that involves developing a nurturing and compassionate relationship with yourself. It is about embracing your worthiness, accepting your flaws and imperfections, and treating yourself with kindness and understanding. Here's a detailed explanation of how to cultivate self-compassion and self-love:

- Recognize Your Inherent Worth: Understand that you are inherently worthy and deserving of love and compassion simply by being human. Recognize that your worth is not dependent on external achievements, validation from others, or meeting unrealistic expectations.

- Practice Self-Acceptance: Embrace all aspects of yourself, including your strengths, weaknesses, and perceived flaws. Accept yourself as a whole, acknowledging that you are a unique and imperfect human being. Let go of self-judgment and cultivate a sense of self-acceptance.

- Be Kind to Yourself: Treat yourself with kindness, gentleness, and understanding. Offer yourself the same care and support you would provide to a loved one going through a difficult time. Use compassionate self-talk and replace self-criticism with self-encouragement and affirmation.

- Practice Self-Compassion: Cultivate self-compassion by acknowledging and validating your own pain, suffering, and challenges. Rather than dismissing or suppressing your emotions, offer yourself empathy and understanding. Recognize that it is natural to experience pain and struggle, and respond with self-compassion in these moments.

- Let Go of Perfectionism: Release the need for perfection and embrace your authentic self. Understand that perfection is an unrealistic standard that can lead to self-criticism and dissatisfaction. Embrace your imperfections as part of what makes you human and focus on growth and self-improvement instead.

- Set Boundaries and Prioritize Self-Care: Honor your own needs and boundaries by setting healthy limits in your relationships, work, and personal life. Prioritize self-care practices that nourish your physical, emotional, and mental well-being. Recognize that taking care of yourself is not selfish but essential for your overall health and happiness.

- Practice Mindfulness: Engage in mindfulness practices to cultivate self-awareness and present-moment acceptance. Observe your thoughts, emotions, and sensations without judgment or attachment. Through mindfulness, you can cultivate a compassionate and non-reactive stance towards yourself.

- Let Go of Comparison: Avoid comparing yourself to others, as it can undermine your self-worth and breed feelings of inadequacy. Focus on your own journey and celebrate your progress, accomplishments, and unique qualities. Embrace the concept of "comparison-free zones" and surround yourself with people and environments that support your growth and self-acceptance.

- Celebrate Your Achievements: Acknowledge and celebrate your accomplishments, no matter how small they may seem. Recognize your efforts, progress, and resilience. By celebrating your achievements, you reinforce a positive self-image and cultivate a sense of self-pride.

- Seek Support and Connection: Reach out for support when needed and cultivate connections with others who uplift and support your journey towards self-compassion and self-love. Surround yourself with people who appreciate and value you for who you are.

Embrace Self-Forgiveness

Practice forgiving yourself for past mistakes and perceived shortcomings. Understand that everyone makes mistakes and that they do not define your worth as a person. Release any guilt or shame you may be carrying and offer yourself forgiveness and understanding.

Nurture Your Inner Child

Connect with your inner child and provide the care, love, and attention they may have missed during your upbringing. Engage in activities that bring joy, playfulness, and creativity. Take time to listen to your inner child's needs and desires, and respond to them with compassion and understanding.

Practice Gratitude

Cultivate gratitude for yourself and your journey. Acknowledge and appreciate your strengths, talents, and unique qualities. Regularly reflect on the things you are grateful for, both internally and externally, and develop a gratitude practice that helps shift your focus towards self-appreciation.

Challenge Negative Self-Talk

Become aware of negative self-talk patterns and challenge them with more positive and compassionate thoughts. Replace self-critical statements with kind and supportive affirmations. Remember, you have the power to change your self-talk and cultivate a more compassionate inner dialogue.

Engage in Self-Reflection

Take time for self-reflection to gain deeper insights into your emotions, thoughts, and behaviors. Reflect on patterns or beliefs that may be hindering your self-compassion and self-love. Use journaling or meditation to explore your inner landscape and cultivate self-awareness.

Practice Self-Compassionate Action

Extend self-compassion beyond thoughts and words by engaging in self-compassionate actions. Treat yourself with acts of kindness, such as taking breaks when needed, engaging in activities that bring you joy, setting healthy boundaries, and prioritizing your well-being.

Surround Yourself with Positive Influences

Surround yourself with people who support and uplift you. Seek out relationships that encourage self-compassion and self-love. Distance yourself from toxic relationships or environments that undermine your self-worth.

Embody Self-Care as a Lifestyle

Integrate self-care practices into your daily life as an ongoing commitment to yourself. Make choices that prioritize your well-being, such as nourishing your body with healthy food, engaging in regular exercise, getting enough rest, and engaging in activities that replenish your energy.

Celebrate Self-Discovery and Growth

Embrace personal growth and the journey of self-discovery. Celebrate the progress you make, no matter how small. Recognize that growth is not linear and that setbacks are opportunities for learning and resilience.

Continuously Revisit and Reinforce

Regularly revisit and reinforce your self-compassion and self-love practices. Allow them to evolve and adapt as you grow and change. Stay committed to nurturing yourself with kindness and understanding, even in challenging times.

4.5 Workbook: Daily Practices For Reparenting Your Inner Child

Reparenting your inner child is a process of providing the care, love, and support that may have been missing during your childhood. It involves nurturing your inner child's emotional needs and creating a safe and loving space within yourself. The following are some daily practices that can help you in this journey:

Exercises	Explanation
Morning Intention Setting	Start your day by setting an intention to connect with and care for your inner child. This can be done through a simple affirmation or statement of love and support. For example, "Today, I commit to loving and nurturing my inner child with compassion and understanding."
Inner Child Check-In	Take a few moments each morning to check in with your inner child. Close your eyes, take deep breaths, and tune into your emotions and sensations. Notice any feelings or needs that arise and offer them acceptance and validation. Ask your inner child how they are feeling and what they need from you today.
Daily Affirmations	Use positive affirmations throughout the day to reinforce self-love and support for your inner child. Repeat affirmations such as, "I am worthy of love and care," "I am enough just as I am," or "I am a loving and nurturing parent to my inner child."
Inner Child Visualization	Engage in a visualization exercise to connect with your inner child. Close your eyes, imagine your inner child, and visualize yourself embracing them with love and compassion. Offer comforting words and gestures of care, such as hugging, holding hands, or offering a gentle smile.
Journaling	Set aside time each day for journaling to explore and express your thoughts and emotions. Write a letter to your inner child, allowing them to express themselves freely and openly. Reflect on your experiences, insights, and any

	challenges you may be facing in your journey of reparenting.
Self-Care Rituals	Incorporate self-care rituals into your daily routine that nurture your inner child's needs. Engage in activities that bring you joy, such as painting, dancing, singing, or spending time in nature. Prioritize activities that provide comfort, relaxation, and a sense of playfulness.
Emotional Expression	Create a safe space for emotional expression. Allow yourself to feel and process your emotions without judgment. Cry, laugh, or express yourself through creative outlets. Remind yourself that all emotions are valid and deserve acknowledgment and understanding.
Boundaries and Self-Protection	Set healthy boundaries to protect your inner child. Identify situations, people, or environments that may trigger your inner child's wounds and practice self-compassion by limiting exposure to them. Establish boundaries that honor your well-being and prioritize your emotional safety.
Positive Self-Talk	Cultivate a positive and nurturing inner dialogue. Replace self-critical thoughts with gentle and supportive self-talk. Offer words of encouragement, reassurance, and validation to your inner child. Remind yourself of your inherent worthiness and loveability.
Evening Reflection	Before bed, take a few moments to reflect on your day and your interactions with your inner child. Celebrate moments of self-care and compassion. Acknowledge any challenges or areas for growth. Offer gratitude for the progress you have made in reparenting your inner child.

Chapter 5: Inner Child Integration

In this chapter, we will explore the concept of inner child integration—a transformative process that allows us to merge our adult self with our healed and nurtured inner child. Through this integration, we can experience profound healing, self-discovery, and an authentic way of living.

5.1 Integrating The Healed Inner Child Into Your Adult Self

Integrating the healed inner child into your adult self is the process of merging the wisdom, healing, and resilience gained from reparenting your inner child with your present-day adult self. It involves bringing the strengths, insights, and emotional well-being of your inner child into your everyday life. Here's a detailed explanation of how to integrate the healed inner child into your adult self:

Recognize Your Inner Child's Gifts

Acknowledge and appreciate the positive qualities and strengths that your inner child embodies. Reflect on the resilience, creativity, joy, curiosity, and authenticity that may have been present during your childhood. Recognize that these qualities are still within you and can be integrated into your adult life.

Embrace Inner Child's Wisdom

Your inner child carries valuable wisdom and intuition. Cultivate a sense of openness and receptivity to the insights and intuition that arise from your inner child. Trust the messages and guidance that emerge, as they can provide valuable perspectives and inform your decisions in the present.

Connect with Joy and Playfulness

Engage in activities that bring out your inner child's sense of joy, playfulness, and spontaneity. Allow yourself to experience moments of lightness, laughter, and fun. Engaging in creative pursuits, exploring hobbies, or spending time with loved ones in a carefree manner can help foster this integration.

Practice Self-Expression

Encourage self-expression in various forms to honor your inner child's need for authenticity. Engage in creative outlets such as writing, drawing, dancing, or singing. Express your emotions openly and honestly, allowing your inner child's voice to be heard and validated.

Embody Emotional Freedom

Allow yourself to fully experience and express a range of emotions without judgment or suppression. Give space to your inner child's emotions and honor their validity. By embracing your emotions and processing them in healthy ways, you can cultivate emotional freedom and resilience.

Nourish Your Inner Child's Needs

Continuously meet the emotional needs of your inner child as they arise. Prioritize self-care practices, set healthy boundaries, and engage in activities that fulfill your inner child's needs for love, safety, connection, and play. By consistently tending to these needs, you provide a nurturing environment for your inner child to thrive.

Practice Self-Compassion

Extend self-compassion to both your adult self and your inner child. Treat yourself with kindness, understanding, and forgiveness. Offer compassion to any wounds or vulnerabilities that arise and remind yourself that you are deserving of love, care, and acceptance.

Embrace Inner Child's Presence

Invite your inner child's presence into your daily life. Cultivate a sense of curiosity and wonder as you navigate the world around you. Allow your inner child's perspective to inform your interactions, decisions, and relationships. Embrace a sense of lightheartedness and awe in your experiences.

Set Healthy Boundaries

Establish healthy boundaries to protect your inner child and honor their needs. Say no to situations or people that may trigger old wounds or compromise your well-being. Advocate for your inner child's safety, emotional well-being, and authentic expression.

Maintain Self-Reflection and Growth

Continuously engage in self-reflection and personal growth practices. Regularly check in with yourself and assess the integration of your healed inner child into your adult self. Identify areas for further growth, healing, and alignment. Be open to continued learning and evolving in your journey.

Healing Core Beliefs

As you continue to work on reparenting and healing your inner child, you may uncover deep-seated core beliefs that were formed during childhood. These beliefs may have shaped your perception of yourself and the world. Integration involves challenging and replacing any negative or limiting beliefs with more empowering and supportive ones. By recognizing and changing these core beliefs, you can align your adult self with the healed perspective of your inner child.

Embracing Vulnerability

Integrating your healed inner child also means embracing vulnerability. Your inner child carries vulnerability and authenticity, and by allowing yourself to be vulnerable, you open the door to deeper connections and emotional intimacy with others. It means showing up as your authentic self, expressing your needs and emotions, and being open to receiving love and support.

Cultivating Inner Strength

The healing journey of your inner child strengthens your resilience and inner strength. As you integrate the healed aspects of your inner child into your adult self, you can tap into this strength in facing life's challenges. You develop a greater sense of self-confidence, assertiveness, and the ability to navigate difficulties with compassion and grace.

Practicing Self-Love

Integration involves deepening your practice of self-love and self-care. It means consistently prioritizing your well-being, setting healthy boundaries, and nurturing yourself physically, emotionally, mentally, and spiritually. By practicing self-love, you reinforce the connection with your inner child and create a foundation of self-worth and self-acceptance.

Embodying Playfulness and Curiosity

Your healed inner child brings forth a sense of playfulness, curiosity, and wonder. Integration involves embodying these qualities in your adult life. Engage in activities that spark joy, embrace curiosity, and encourage exploration. By infusing playfulness into your daily experiences, you invite a sense of lightness and enjoyment into your life.

Embracing Inner Guidance

Integration means learning to trust and follow your inner guidance, which is often a reflection of your healed inner child's wisdom. Listen to your intuition and inner voice, and make choices that align with your authentic self. By honoring and acting upon your inner guidance, you align your adult self with the values and desires of your inner child.

Embracing Imperfection

Integration involves embracing the imperfections of both your adult self and your inner child. Recognize that growth and healing are ongoing processes, and it's okay to make mistakes or have setbacks. Embrace the journey with compassion and patience, knowing that each step forward brings you closer to wholeness and integration.

Sharing Your Healing Journey

Integration may also involve sharing your healing journey with others. By sharing your experiences, insights, and wisdom gained from reparenting your inner child, you can inspire and support others on their own healing journeys. Additionally, it reinforces the integration of your healed inner child into your adult self as you embody and expresses your authentic self in the world.

5.2 Embracing The Gifts And Strengths Of Your Inner Child

Embracing the gifts and strengths of your inner child is an essential part of healing and integrating your inner child into your adult self. Your inner child carries unique qualities and strengths that can enhance your life and bring joy, creativity, and authenticity to your experiences. Here's a detailed explanation of how to embrace the gifts and strengths of your inner child:

Recognize Your Inner Child's Qualities

Take time to reflect on the positive qualities and strengths that your inner child embodies. These may include traits such as creativity, curiosity, resilience, spontaneity, playfulness, and authenticity. Acknowledge and appreciate these qualities as valuable contributions to who you are as a person.

Cultivate Self-Acceptance

Embrace self-acceptance by honoring and embracing all aspects of yourself, including the qualities and strengths of your inner child. Recognize that these qualities are a part of your essence and make you unique. Embrace the diversity within yourself and celebrate the gifts that your inner child brings to your adult self.

Engage in Play and Creativity

Allow yourself to engage in activities that foster play and creativity. Tap into your inner child's sense of wonder and imagination. Engaging in playful activities, hobbies, or creative outlets such as painting, dancing, writing, or playing an instrument can help you reconnect with the joyful and expressive nature of your inner child.

Trust Your Intuition

Your inner child often carries a sense of intuition and wisdom. Embrace and trust your intuition as it arises. This intuitive guidance can help you make decisions that align with your authentic self and lead to positive outcomes. Allow your inner child's wisdom to guide you in various areas of your life, from relationships to career choices.

Embrace Spontaneity

Embrace spontaneity in your life by allowing yourself to let go of rigid routines and expectations. Be open to new experiences, unexpected adventures, and moments of joyful spontaneity. Embracing the spontaneous nature of your inner child can bring excitement, novelty, and a sense of freedom into your life.

Foster Creativity and Imagination

Nurture your creative side and tap into your imagination. Engage in activities that encourage creativity, such as writing, drawing, crafting, or brainstorming new ideas. Give yourself permission to explore and express your inner child's imaginative ideas without judgment or self-censorship.

Cultivate Joy and Laughter

Embrace joy and laughter as essential aspects of your life. Seek out experiences, people, and activities that bring you genuine joy and make you laugh. Surround yourself with positive and uplifting energy that nourishes your inner child's need for joy and happiness.

Embody Authenticity

Allow your inner child's authenticity to shine through in your interactions and relationships. Be true to yourself and express your thoughts, feelings, and desires authentically. Embracing your inner child's authenticity creates genuine connections and fosters a sense of belonging and acceptance.

Embrace Playful Communication

Infuse playfulness and light-heartedness into your communication style. Embrace humor, use playful language, and engage in lighthearted conversations. Embracing a playful communication style can create a positive and joyful atmosphere in your interactions with others.

Practice Self-Care

Prioritize self-care practices that nourish your inner child's needs. Engage in activities that bring you comfort, relaxation, and pleasure. This can include anything from taking baths, spending time in nature, practicing mindfulness, or indulging in activities that bring you joy and relaxation.

Enhancing Creativity and Problem-Solving Skills

Your inner child is naturally imaginative and creative. By embracing and tapping into this aspect of yourself, you can enhance your creativity and problem-solving skills. Your inner child's ability to think outside the box, explore unconventional ideas, and approach challenges with a fresh perspective can lead to innovative solutions and greater success in various areas of your life.

Rediscovering Passion and Purpose

Embracing your inner child's gifts and strengths can help you rediscover your passion and sense of purpose. Your inner child often holds the key to your authentic desires and interests. By reconnecting with those passions and incorporating them into your life, you can experience a greater sense of fulfillment and meaning.

Cultivating Resilience and Adaptability

Your inner child embodies resilience, adaptability, and a natural ability to bounce back from setbacks. By embracing these qualities, you can develop a resilient mindset that helps you navigate challenges and overcome obstacles in life. Embracing your inner child's strengths allows you to approach difficulties with a sense of optimism and an unwavering belief in your ability to overcome adversity.

Bringing Joy and Lightness to Life

Embracing the gifts and strengths of your inner child brings a sense of joy, playfulness, and lightness to your life. It allows you to let go of rigid expectations, perfectionism, and the weight of adulthood responsibilities. By infusing your life with the joy and playfulness of your inner child, you create a more balanced and fulfilling existence.

Strengthening Relationships

Embracing your inner child's gifts and strengths can enhance your relationships with others. The authenticity, creativity, and joy that emanate from your inner child can attract like-minded individuals and foster deeper connections. Your ability to express yourself authentically and engage in playful interactions can create more meaningful and fulfilling relationships.

Inspiring Others

When you embrace the gifts and strengths of your inner child, you become an inspiration to others. Your authenticity, creativity, and resilience can serve as a source of motivation and encouragement for those around you. By embracing your inner child, you give permission for others to do the same and create a ripple effect of healing and growth.

Unleashing Hidden Talents

Your inner child holds a treasure trove of hidden talents and abilities. By embracing your inner child's gifts, you may discover talents and passions that have been dormant or overlooked. This exploration can lead to personal and professional growth as you tap into your full potential and pursue endeavors that align with your authentic self.

Cultivating Self-Discovery and Self-Acceptance

Embracing the gifts and strengths of your inner child is an opportunity for self-discovery and self-acceptance. It allows you to explore and embrace all aspects of yourself, including the playful, creative, and authentic parts that may have been suppressed or neglected. Through this process, you cultivate a deeper understanding and acceptance of yourself, fostering self-love and self-compassion.

5.3 Living Authentically And Joyfully

Living authentically and joyfully is a transformative way of being that allows you to embrace your true self and live a life that aligns with your values, passions, and desires. It is about living from a place of authenticity and finding joy in every aspect of your life. When you live authentically, you no longer seek external validation or approval, but instead, you trust your own intuition and inner guidance.

Living authentically requires self-awareness and introspection. It involves taking the time to explore your beliefs, values, and aspirations. By understanding your true self, you can make choices that resonate with your authentic desires rather than conforming to societal expectations or the opinions of others. This may involve stepping out of your comfort zone, challenging limiting beliefs, and embracing vulnerability.

Authentic living also involves expressing your thoughts, emotions and needs honestly and openly. It means being true to yourself in your relationships and interactions with others, setting boundaries, and communicating assertively. By being authentic in your connections, you build deeper and more meaningful relationships based on trust, understanding, and mutual respect.

Living joyfully is an essential part of authentic living. It means finding joy in the present moment and cultivating a positive outlook on life. It involves appreciating simple pleasures, expressing gratitude, and focusing on the things that bring you happiness. Joy is not dependent on external circumstances but rather arises from within as you embrace the beauty and possibilities of each day.

To live authentically and joyfully, it is important to let go of the need for perfection and embrace imperfection. Accepting yourself fully, including your flaws and mistakes, allows you to release self-judgment and cultivate self-compassion. It is through self-compassion that you can nurture a loving relationship with yourself and embrace your authentic self with kindness and acceptance.

Living authentically and joyfully also requires courage. It may mean making difficult decisions, pursuing your passions, or stepping into new opportunities. It involves embracing uncertainty and being open to growth and change. By living authentically and joyfully, you create a life that is true to yourself, filled with purpose, fulfillment, and genuine happiness.

Living authentically and joyfully is about creating a life that is aligned with your true self, where you can express your values, passions, and desires freely. It involves breaking free from societal expectations, cultural conditioning, and the need for external validation. When you live authentically and joyfully, you tap into your inner wisdom and follow the path that feels right for you, regardless of what others may think or say.

One aspect of living authentically is honoring your own unique journey. Recognize that your path may be different from others', and that's perfectly okay. Embrace your individuality and allow yourself to explore and pursue your own dreams and aspirations. Trust that you have within you the power to create a life that reflects your authentic self.

Living joyfully is closely intertwined with living authentically. When you live from a place of authenticity, you naturally invite more joy into your life. Joy arises from embracing the present moment, finding gratitude for what you have, and engaging in activities that bring you a sense of fulfillment and happiness. It's about cultivating an attitude of positivity and seeking out the beauty and joy in everyday experiences.

To live authentically and joyfully, it is crucial to listen to your inner voice and honor your needs and desires. This involves tuning into your intuition and inner guidance system. Pay attention to the subtle nudges, gut feelings, and inner whispers that guide you toward what is true and meaningful for you. Trusting yourself and making choices that align with your authentic self brings a deep sense of fulfillment and joy.

Living authentically and joyfully also requires self-acceptance and self-compassion. Embrace all aspects of yourself, including your strengths, weaknesses, and past mistakes. Allow yourself to grow and learn from experiences without self-judgment. Treat yourself with kindness and understanding, recognizing that you are deserving of love and joy just as you are.

Furthermore, surrounding yourself with a supportive and nurturing community can greatly enhance your ability to live authentically and joyfully. Seek out relationships and connections that uplift and inspire you. Surround yourself with people who accept and appreciate you for who you truly are and who encourage your personal growth and authenticity.

Living authentically and joyfully is not about denying or suppressing challenging emotions or experiences. It's about acknowledging and embracing the full range of human emotions while consciously choosing to focus on the positive and nurturing aspects of life. This includes engaging in self-care practices that promote your well-being, such as mindfulness, meditation, physical exercise, creative outlets, and spending time in nature.

5.4 Nurturing Ongoing Inner Child Growth And Healing

Nurturing ongoing inner child growth and healing is a deeply personal and transformative process that involves tending to the wounded aspects of ourselves from childhood. The concept of the inner child represents the vulnerable, innocent, and authentic parts of our psyche that may have been wounded or neglected during our early years. By acknowledging and nurturing these wounded aspects, we can cultivate personal growth, healing, and emotional well-being.

The process of nurturing ongoing inner child growth and healing begins with self-awareness and reflection. It requires us to examine our past experiences, beliefs, and patterns of behavior that may have originated from childhood. By gaining a deeper understanding of how our early experiences have shaped us, we can start to identify the wounds and emotional needs that still require attention.

Once we become aware of our inner child's needs, we can begin the process of nurturing and healing. This involves providing the love, care, and support that may have been lacking during our formative years. It's about giving ourselves permission to feel and express our emotions, creating a safe space for self-expression, and cultivating self-compassion.

One powerful way to nurture ongoing inner child growth and healing is through inner child work.

This therapeutic approach involves connecting with the wounded aspects of ourselves and addressing their unmet needs. This can be done through various techniques, such as visualization, journaling, dialogue, or creative expression. By engaging with our inner child, we can offer comfort, validation, and reassurance, helping them heal and integrate into our present selves.

In addition to inner child work, nurturing ongoing inner child growth and healing requires ongoing self-care practices. This can include engaging in activities that bring us joy and playfulness, setting boundaries to protect our emotional well-being, and seeking support from trusted individuals or professionals. It's about creating a nurturing environment for our inner child to thrive and heal.

Nurturing ongoing inner child growth and healing is a lifelong journey. It's not a one-time fix but rather an ongoing commitment to self-discovery and self-care. As we continue to nurture and heal our inner child, we may experience increased self-acceptance, emotional resilience, and a greater capacity for authentic relationships. Ultimately, this process allows us to reclaim our innate wholeness and live more fulfilling lives.

Nurturing ongoing inner child growth and healing is a multifaceted process that encompasses various aspects of our emotional, psychological, and spiritual well-being. It involves delving into the depths of our subconscious mind to address the unresolved issues, traumas, and unmet needs that originated from our childhood experiences.

One key aspect of nurturing ongoing inner child growth and healing is developing self-compassion. Often, the wounds of our inner child stem from experiences of neglect, rejection, or emotional pain. By cultivating self-compassion, we learn to treat ourselves with kindness, understanding, and empathy. We acknowledge that the wounds we carry are not our fault, and we deserve love and healing.

Another important element is re-parenting our inner child. This involves assuming the role of a nurturing and supportive parent to ourselves. We learn to provide the love, guidance, and validation that may have been missing in our early years. Through self-soothing techniques, self-care rituals, and inner dialogue, we offer the reassurance and emotional support our inner child needs to heal and grow.

As we engage in nurturing ongoing inner child growth and healing, it is common to encounter resistance, discomfort, and even painful emotions. This is a normal part of the healing process, as we are confronting and releasing buried emotions and beliefs. It is crucial to create a safe and non-judgmental space for ourselves, allowing these emotions to arise and be processed without self-criticism or suppression.

In addition to inner work, it can be beneficial to seek support from therapists, counselors, or support groups specializing in inner child healing. These professionals can provide guidance, tools, and a safe space for exploring and healing the wounds of our inner child. They can assist us in uncovering deeper layers of emotional pain and help us navigate the healing process with greater clarity and understanding.

It's important to note that nurturing ongoing inner child growth and healing is not about dwelling solely on the past. While acknowledging and addressing our childhood wounds is a vital part of the process, the ultimate goal is to integrate our healed inner child into our present selves. By doing so, we cultivate a greater sense of wholeness and authenticity, enabling us to live more fulfilling and joyful lives.

5.5 Reflecting On Your Inner Child Healing Journey

Reflecting on your inner child's healing journey is an essential aspect of the healing process. It involves taking the time to pause, introspect, and gain insight into the progress you have made, the challenges you have faced, and the growth you have experienced. This reflective practice allows you to deepen your understanding of yourself, celebrate your accomplishments, and identify areas that may require further attention and healing.

One aspect of reflecting on your inner child healing journey is acknowledging the progress you have made. It's important to recognize and honor the steps you have taken to nurture and heal your inner child. Consider the inner work you have engaged in, the therapy or healing modalities you have pursued, and the changes you have noticed in your emotional well-being and patterns of behavior. Recognizing your growth and the positive shifts you have experienced can be incredibly empowering and motivating.

Reflecting on your inner child healing journey also involves exploring the challenges you have encountered along the way. Healing deep emotional wounds can be a complex and sometimes challenging process. It's important to acknowledge any setbacks, emotional triggers, or difficult emotions that have arisen during your healing journey. By shining a light on these challenges, you can gain insight into the areas that still require attention and explore strategies to navigate and overcome them.

In addition to recognizing progress and challenges, reflecting on your inner child healing journey allows you to connect with the emotions and memories that arise during the process. As you delve into the depths of your inner child's wounds, you may encounter feelings of sadness, anger, grief, or fear. Reflecting on these emotions and the memories associated with them helps you validate and process them. It allows you to offer yourself the compassion and support needed for continued healing and growth.

Reflection also involves exploring the connections between your past and present experiences. By reflecting on your inner child healing journey, you may notice patterns or recurring themes that stem from your childhood. These patterns may manifest in your relationships, self-esteem, or behavioral patterns. Gaining awareness of these connections allows you to make conscious choices and break free from repetitive cycles that no longer serve you.

Moreover, reflecting on your inner child healing journey invites you to assess your self-care practices and identify areas for improvement. Taking care of yourself on a physical, emotional, and spiritual level is crucial for ongoing healing and growth. Reflect on the self-care rituals, boundaries, and activities that have supported your well-being. Consider if there are any adjustments or additions you can make to further nurture yourself and create a safe and loving space for your inner child.

Finally, reflecting on your inner child healing journey is an opportunity to express gratitude for the progress you have made and the support you have received. Gratitude cultivates a positive mindset and acknowledges the interconnectedness of your healing journey with the individuals, resources, and experiences that have contributed to your growth. By expressing gratitude, you reinforce a sense of abundance and resilience, fostering a mindset that supports further healing and transformation.

Reflecting on your inner child healing journey involves creating dedicated time and space for introspection and self-inquiry. This can be done through journaling, meditation, therapy sessions, or engaging in creative activities that allow you to explore your thoughts and emotions. By setting aside this intentional time, you give yourself the opportunity to delve deeper into your healing process and gain valuable insights.

During the reflection process, it can be helpful to consider specific moments or experiences that have been significant in your healing journey. Think about pivotal breakthroughs, moments of clarity, or instances where you felt a deep sense of connection with your inner child. Reflecting on these moments allows you to appreciate the profound shifts that have occurred and reinforces your commitment to continued healing.

As you reflect, it's essential to be gentle with yourself and practice self-compassion. Healing inner child wounds can be challenging and may bring up intense emotions. It's normal to experience moments of frustration, resistance, or impatience. By approaching yourself with kindness and understanding, you create a supportive environment that encourages healing and growth.

Part of reflecting on your inner child healing journey involves identifying any recurring patterns or beliefs that you have become aware of throughout the process. These patterns may manifest in your relationships, self-perception, or ways of coping with difficult emotions. By recognizing these patterns, you gain the opportunity to consciously choose alternative responses and break free from cycles that no longer serve you.

In addition to looking inward, reflection also involves acknowledging the external resources and support systems that have contributed to your healing journey. This can include therapists, mentors, support groups, or loved ones who have provided guidance, understanding, and encouragement. Expressing gratitude for their presence and impact can deepen your appreciation for the collaborative nature of healing and remind you of the interconnectedness of your journey.

Furthermore, reflecting on your inner child healing journey allows you to reassess and refine your self-care practices. Take the time to evaluate the activities, rituals, and habits that have supported your well-being and connection with your inner child. Consider if there are any adjustments or new practices that you can incorporate to further nurture yourself. Self-care is an ongoing process, and reflection helps you ensure that your practices align with your evolving needs.

Lastly, reflection provides an opportunity for integration and celebration. Take a moment to acknowledge and celebrate the progress you have made on your healing journey. Recognize the strength, resilience, and courage that you have demonstrated throughout the process. By celebrating your growth, you reinforce a positive mindset and cultivate a sense of empowerment as you continue on your path of inner child healing.

5.6 Encouragement And Next Steps

Encouragement and next steps play a crucial role in the process of inner child healing. As you engage in this transformative journey, it's important to provide yourself with ongoing encouragement and support. This helps to maintain motivation, resilience, and a sense of progress. Additionally, identifying and planning your next steps allows you to continue nurturing your inner child and fostering lasting healing and growth.

Encouragement serves as a source of motivation and self-validation throughout the inner child healing process. Acknowledge the progress you have made so far, no matter how small or significant. Celebrate your achievements, breakthroughs, and moments of self-discovery. By recognizing your efforts and the positive changes that have occurred, you reinforce a sense of accomplishment and self-belief.

It can be helpful to cultivate a compassionate inner dialogue, speaking to yourself with kindness and understanding. Offer words of encouragement and affirmation when faced with challenges or setbacks. Remind yourself of your resilience and the strength you have demonstrated on your healing journey. This self-encouragement helps to counteract self-doubt and fuels your motivation to continue the healing process.

The next steps are the actions and strategies you plan to implement to sustain your inner child healing journey. These steps may involve various aspects, including further self-reflection, continued therapy or counseling sessions, exploring new healing modalities, or integrating self-care practices into your daily routine. The specific next steps will vary for each individual, depending on their unique needs and circumstances.

To determine your next steps, reflect on the areas that still require attention and growth in your inner child healing process. Consider the patterns, beliefs, or triggers that continue to affect you and identify specific actions that can help address them. Seek support from therapists, coaches, or mentors who specialize in inner child healing to guide you in formulating an effective plan.

Integrating self-care practices is a vital aspect of the next steps in your inner child healing journey. Self-care nourishes and nurtures your inner child, fostering an environment of safety, love, and healing. Identify self-care activities that resonate with you and incorporate them into your routine consistently. This can include engaging in hobbies you enjoy, practicing mindfulness or meditation, setting healthy boundaries, or seeking social support.

It's essential to approach your next steps with patience and self-compassion. Healing is a gradual process, and it's natural to encounter setbacks or challenges along the way. Be gentle with yourself and understand that progress may not always be linear. Adjust your expectations and embrace the journey, knowing that each step, no matter how small, contributes to your overall healing and growth.

Regularly reassess your next steps to ensure they align with your evolving needs. Inner child healing is a dynamic process, and your requirements may change over time. Stay open to exploring new possibilities and adjusting your approach as necessary. Be willing to seek additional support or guidance when needed, and be open to learning from your experiences.

Encouragement is a vital aspect of the inner child healing journey. It involves providing yourself with positive reinforcement, support, and validation for the progress you have made. Inner child healing can be challenging, as it often involves confronting deep emotional wounds and facing difficult memories. Encouragement helps to counteract self-doubt, fear, and the internal critical voice that may arise during the process.

One way to offer encouragement is by acknowledging and celebrating your achievements, no matter how small they may seem. Reflect on the breakthrough moments, insights, and positive changes you have experienced. This can include moments of self-awareness, improved emotional regulation, healthier coping mechanisms, or enhanced self-compassion. By recognizing and celebrating these achievements, you reinforce your belief in your capacity for healing and growth.

Another aspect of encouragement is cultivating self-compassion. Inner child healing often involves revisiting painful memories and emotions, which can evoke feelings of vulnerability or shame. It's important to approach yourself with kindness, understanding, and acceptance during these moments. Offer yourself words of encouragement, reminding yourself that the healing journey requires courage and vulnerability. Treat yourself as you would a dear friend, providing support and reassurance along the way.

Encouragement can also be fostered through engaging in a supportive community. Seek out individuals who understand and support your inner child healing journey. This can include friends, family members, therapists, support groups, or online communities. Connecting with others who have similar experiences or are on a similar healing path can provide validation, understanding, and encouragement. Sharing your challenges, victories, and insights with others who can empathize can be empowering and inspiring.

The next steps refer to the actions and strategies you plan to take to continue nurturing your inner child and fostering ongoing healing and growth. Identifying your next steps is a proactive approach to sustaining progress and ensuring that you continue to prioritize your inner child's needs. These steps will be unique to your individual healing journey and should align with your specific goals and circumstances.

To determine your next steps, engage in self-reflection and introspection. Consider the areas in which you feel there is still healing or growth needed. Reflect on patterns, triggers, or beliefs that continue to impact your well-being. This self-awareness can help you identify specific actions or areas of focus that will contribute to your continued healing.

The next steps may involve various aspects of healing, such as ongoing therapy or counseling sessions to explore deeper layers of trauma or emotional wounds. You may choose to incorporate new healing modalities, such as energy work, art therapy, or somatic practices, to further address and release stored emotions. Alternatively, your next steps may involve integrating self-care practices more consistently into your daily life to support your emotional well-being and nourish your inner child.

Regularly reassessing and adjusting your next steps is important as your healing journey evolves. Inner child healing is a dynamic process, and your needs may change over time. Stay open to new possibilities and be willing to explore different approaches or seek additional support if necessary. It's essential to be flexible and adaptable, as your healing journey is unique to you and may require different strategies at different stages.

Remember to approach your next steps with patience and self-compassion. Healing is not a linear process, and setbacks or challenges may arise along the way. Be gentle with yourself and understand that progress takes time. Embrace the journey, knowing that every step you take, no matter how small, contributes to your overall healing and growth.

5.7 Workbook: Creating A Personalized Inner Child Integration Plan

Creating a personalized inner child integration plan involves designing a structured approach to healing, nurturing, and integrating your inner child into your adult self. This workbook acts as a guide to help you develop a plan tailored to your unique needs and circumstances. Here's a detailed explanation of the components and benefits of creating a personalized inner child integration plan:

Exercises	Explanation
Self-Reflection and Assessment	The first step in creating a personalized inner child integration plan is to engage in self-reflection and assessment. Take time to explore your childhood experiences, identify any unresolved wounds or traumas, and reflect on how they may have impacted your present life. This self-awareness allows you to better understand your inner child's needs and informs the subsequent steps in your integration plan.

Setting Goals and Intentions	Once you have gained clarity through self-reflection, it's important to set goals and intentions for your inner child integration journey. These goals can include healing specific wounds, cultivating self-compassion, developing healthier coping mechanisms, or improving relationships. Clearly defining your goals provides direction and motivation for your inner child's healing process.
Identifying Healing Practices	The next step is to identify specific healing practices that resonate with you and support your inner child's growth and healing. These practices can include therapeutic techniques such as journaling, meditation, art therapy, inner child dialogues, or seeking professional help. Consider your personal preferences, resources, and availability when selecting the healing practices that will be included in your integration plan.
Creating a Healing Schedule	Developing a healing schedule is crucial for consistency and accountability in your inner child integration journey. Determine how often you will engage in healing practices and allocate specific time slots in your daily or weekly routine. This schedule ensures that you prioritize your inner child's needs and dedicate regular time and effort to their healing and integration.
Establishing Supportive Structures	Building a supportive structure around your inner child integration plan is essential for success. This can involve seeking support from loved ones, joining support groups or therapy sessions, or connecting with online communities focused on inner child healing. Having a support system provides validation, encouragement, and guidance throughout your journey.
Tracking Progress and Adjusting	Regularly monitoring your progress is important to stay motivated and make adjustments as needed. Keep a journal or use a tracking system to record your experiences,

	insights, and growth. This helps you identify patterns, celebrate achievements, and make necessary modifications to your integration plan based on your evolving needs.
Self-Care and Self-Compassion	Integrating self-care and self-compassion into your plan is crucial for nurturing your inner child's healing process. Incorporate self-care practices that nourish your physical, emotional, mental, and spiritual well-being. Practice self-compassion by treating yourself with kindness, understanding, and patience throughout your journey. This creates a nurturing and supportive environment for your inner child to heal and thrive.
Celebration and Reflection	Regularly take time to celebrate your progress and reflect on your journey. Acknowledge the milestones, breakthroughs, and personal growth you have experienced. Celebrating your achievements reinforces positive changes and motivates you to continue nurturing and integrating your inner child.

By creating a personalized inner child integration plan, you establish a structured and intentional framework for your healing journey. This plan empowers you to address specific needs, set clear goals, implement healing practices, and stay committed to your inner child's growth and integration. It provides a roadmap for navigating the complexities of inner child healing and ensures that you prioritize your well-being and nurture the relationship with your inner child.

Conclusion

Congratulations on completing your journey through "Unlocking the Healing of the Inner Child." You have taken significant steps toward healing and nurturing your inner child, and your commitment to this process is commendable. As you reflect on the insights and exercises shared throughout this book, remember that healing is a lifelong journey—a continuous process of self-discovery and growth.

Throughout this book, you have gained a deeper understanding of the inner child, its wounds, and the profound impact they have on your adult life. By reconnecting with your inner child, you have begun to provide the love, care, and validation it needs to heal. You have recognized the power of acknowledging and processing childhood wounds, releasing emotional pain, and embracing forgiveness and compassion for yourself and others.

The journey of healing the inner child is not without its challenges, but the rewards are immeasurable. As you continue to reparent your inner child, providing the care and support it needs, you are paving the way for a more authentic and fulfilling life. Through setting healthy boundaries, cultivating self-compassion, and embracing your inner child's gifts and strengths, you are reclaiming your power and embracing a newfound sense of joy and wholeness.

Remember, this is not the end but rather a new beginning. The healing of your inner child is an ongoing process that requires patience, commitment, and self-compassion. As you move forward, be gentle with yourself. Celebrate your progress, no matter how small, and acknowledge the courage it takes to face and heal your past wounds.

In addition to the tools and exercises provided in this book, remember that there are many resources available to support you on your healing journey. Seek out therapy, support groups, or additional reading materials that resonate with you. Surround yourself with a supportive community that understands the importance of inner child healing.

Finally, I want to express my gratitude for allowing me to be a part of your healing journey. It has been an honor to guide you through this transformative process. As you move forward, may you continue to nurture and honor your inner child, cultivating a life filled with love, authenticity, and joy.

Embrace the wisdom and resilience of your inner child. Unlock the healing that lies within and create a future that is guided by compassion, understanding, and self-love. Your inner child deserves a life filled with happiness, and by unlocking their healing, you are opening the doors to a world of endless possibilities.

Remember, you are worthy of love, healing, and a life filled with joy. May your journey of healing the inner child continue to bring you profound transformation and an abundance of inner peace.

Frame the qr code to download the workbook and start your adventure (let me know if it helped you)

deborah.f.blane@gmail.com

Review this book

Thank you for reading this far! I would be extremely grateful if you would take a minute of your time to leave an honest review of my work on Amazon.

To review the book frame the QR code

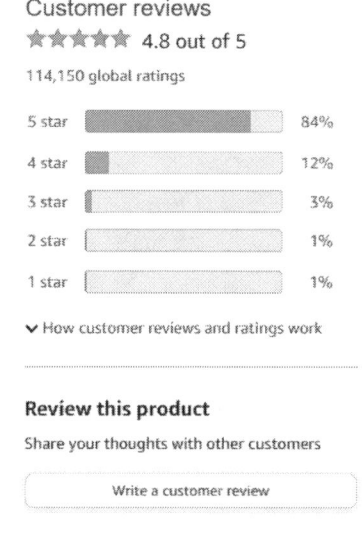

Made in United States
Orlando, FL
02 January 2024